THROUGH TEARS AND LAUGHTER

Phyllis Ing

Through Tears and Laughter

Phyllis Ing

Through Tears And Laughter

Phyllis Ing

AVON COURT PRESS

First published 2006

by Avon Court Press
24 Avon Court
Mold, Flints CH7 1JP

Copyright Phyllis Ing

Printed by Proprint
13 The Metro Centre, Welbeck Way, Peterborough,
Cambs PE2 7UH

ISBN10: 0 95538 10 0 2
ISBN13: 978 09553810 0 3

1

1910-1915

Phyllis (left) and Muriel (right) aged one year; behind (left to right) Bill, May and Bert

"My God, what have we done to deserve this?" These were the words spoken by our maternal Grandfather Varnham on hearing of the birth of my twin sister and me; not surprisingly seeing that the year before my Aunt Edie had also presented him with twin granddaughters. It was hardly the way to welcome two little innocents into the world. When we were born in 1910 we already had two brothers and a sister and eighteen months after our arrival we had another sister. Three years later our youngest was born, the last member of the family, making seven of us in all. William (Will) was the eldest, then Albert (Bert) followed by May. We came next, Muriel and me (Phyllis), then Ethel, and Frank was the youngest. We were a very happy family, both Mother and Father, Beatrice and William Eaton, had a keen sense of humour, which they passed onto all of us. This stood us in good stead later on in life. Father was a solicitor's managing clerk, which in those days, in the early part of the century, was a good job to have. We lived in a big house, in Wood Green in north London, with a fairly large garden, of which Dada, as we called him, was very proud. Both our parents were very musical, Dada played the organ and violin and Mother the piano. Dada used to sing a lot of comic songs, his Father had been an opera singer. We did not remember him because he died when we were very young and Grandmother, Dada's mother, died when he was a boy.

In later years Mother would tell us of things that happened when we were young, such as the time she made a roly-poly pudding for our dinner but when she came to put it in the pot, she could not find it anywhere. After looking high and low, she looked out of the window and saw Ethel, then aged two, walking around in the garden with the pudding in her arms calling out to the neighbours to look at her new dolly. One day Mother took us, all six (before Frank was born) to the pictures, of course the silent ones. Ethel must have been watching the film intently because suddenly in a loud voice she shouted out, "Put that poor pussy down you naughty man." Apparently the man was stealing the cat. Mother said the place was in an uproar.

I remember one day I had hiccoughs, so Will said he knew a cure for that. Of course being 'big brother' I took his word for it. He gave me a nasturtium seed to eat. Needless to say it burned my mouth and I screamed. Mother came rushing out to see what the trouble was. Seeing what had happened she was very cross with Will and gave him a spanking, something she very rarely did. If there was any argument among us Mother or Dada would soon sort us out, we were never allowed to quarrel; this was a good foundation for our later life. Will always had a sweet tooth; he still had at the age of ninety-one. One day he saw a tin of condensed milk in the cupboard. He decided to help himself to a spoonful - fine, until Dada found a trail of milk all around the kitchen floor. Will did get the cane for that! Another day May picked all the heads off Dada's prize poppies. Mother said she made sure May was in bed before Dada came home. One Sunday afternoon Mother and Dada wanted a bit of peace and quiet, so they told Will to take the rest of us to the park for an hour. Mother said we had not been gone long before they heard such a commotion in the street and looking out of the window she saw a policeman carrying Ethel in his arms and the rest of us, as well as a number of other children, following on behind. On opening the door she saw Ethel was soaking wet, in a very loud voice Ethel said, "A big doggie pushed me into the pond and I've got a snotty nose." As luck would have it she was none the worse for her adventure.

We loved the weekends when Dada was home and he had more time to play with us. Sometimes Mother and Dada would give us a musical evening playing the violin, piano and singing. Although I was very young I can still remember those times. Mother's parents lived in Dalston, in north-east London, and every so often Mother would take us on the bus to visit them. How we loved those outings. One day when Mother took us out the bus conductor said if she could prove we were all hers we could travel for nothing, because we were so well behaved. Another day when Dada came home from work he asked the usual question, how we had all been today, Mother replied, "Little devils!" Apparently Dada was shocked at her remark and said, "Don't ever call our children little devils." I think Mother told him he should be with us all day!

When we were four years old we went to school in White Hart Lane, Tottenham. I remember that first day very well. I stood and wet the floor and May had to take me home to get some dry clothes. Mother was not cross with me because she knew my weakness. Right from birth I was much weaker than Muriel, she thrived on anything but Mother had an awful job rearing me.

I do not remember anything of the first year of the war but 1915 was the year that changed all our lives. When the war broke out Dada tried to get into the Royal Flying Corps but he was rejected because of poor eyesight. Soon afterwards he became ill and was diagnosed as having Addison's disease, in those days incurable. Dada knew this, and two weeks before Muriel and I were five, he died.

In spite of his remark at the beginning of my story Grandpa was really very fond of us all, so much so that he and Grandma took us all into their home, after Dada's death. That Christmas, as far as we children were concerned was a very happy one, but little did we know it would be twelve years before we would be celebrating the festive season together as a family again. Whether our parents and grandparents had talked things over before Dada's death I do not know, somehow I imagine so. Within six weeks of Dada's death Muriel and I were in an orphanage and our world fell apart.

2

1916-1918

"Bye-bye darlings, be good girls and I will see you again soon." Mother gave us a kiss and left the room, closing the door quietly behind her. Muriel and I were standing in the middle of a large room, frightened and bewildered by the sea of faces around us. We started to cry uncontrollably. A large woman in a dark frock and a large white apron came towards us. She lifted us up onto a table for every one to see. By now our crying was almost hysterical. "Now children, that will do," she said, "no one is going to hurt you if you do as you are told. Which one of you is Muriel and who is Phyllis?" I pointed towards Muriel and said that is *Moo-moo*, (which is what I called her at home.) The woman remarked, " We don't have silly names here, she will be Muriel from now on." I clung to my sister with tears pouring down both cheeks. "Now that is enough of this crying," the woman said and we were lifted down and stood in front of her. Gradually our sobs subsided and we began to look around. All the little girls were dressed like us in dark blue dresses and white pinafores, long black stockings and black boots. We also noticed that all the girls had their hair cut short like boys. The woman then told us her name was Nurse Springthorpe and we must always call her 'Nurse' whenever we spoke to her. She asked if we understood and we both nodded our heads in agreement. "When the bell goes," Nurse went on "you must line up with the other children to go to the dining hall for tea. You will then be shown to your dormitory, where you will sleep. You must not talk in the corridor or the dining hall. Is that clear?" "Yes, Nurse," we both answered at once. "In the meantime," she said, "you can begin to get to know the other girls." Our life in the orphanage had begun.

Before I continue my story I will tell you about the school itself. It was founded by the Reverend Andrew Reid in 1843 for the children of so-called white-collar workers, clerks, doctors, teachers, etc. The foundation stone was laid by Prince Albert, Queen Victoria's consort. It was situated in East London, at Snaresbrook on the edge of Epping Forest. The building seemed like a huge castle standing in several acres of grounds, next to a lake. It had a very beautiful chapel and swimming pool, also its own Infirmary, later called the Sanatorium. The school took children from six months old to sixteen years. There was a very well equipped nursery. To get admitted to the school every child was voted in. This is where our grandfather worked hard for us. He was a ward beadle to two of the City of London wards, so he knew many influential people. He would visit the big firms in the city and ask for votes. I think £50 kept a child in the school for a year; of course there were other contributions to the school. The orphanage was meant to be a childrens' haven but was called *The Infant Orphanage Asylum*. Doctor Reid said there were places elsewhere for very poor children but nothing was being done for the families of middle-class widows. Later it received the Royal Patronage and became the Royal Infant Orphanage and, later still, the Royal Wanstead School. It finally closed in 1975 and the building now houses the Snaresbrook Crown Courts.

Muriel and I were not in the same dormitory, which upset me very much and I cried myself to sleep. In the morning, on waking, I wanted to go to the toilet and as I had forgotten where it was I began to cry. Nurse got quite cross with me and told one of the girls to take me. Unfortunately I left it too late and wet the floor. Before I knew what had happened I felt a stinging blow on my bottom. "You filthy child," cried the nurse. "We don't have that sort of behaviour here." I was then made to wipe it up. By now I was feeling very sorry for myself, I wanted my *Moo-moo*! During the afternoon Muriel and I had all our curls cut off and we were like all the rest of the girls, more like boys!

Our time of arrival at the orphanage was during the First World War. I cannot remember much about it except that some nights we were roused from our beds and marched down to the cellars. One night one of the girls left her teddy bear in bed and Nurse thought it was a child. She was very cross; I expect she was afraid that one of us was left behind. Anyway, we were never allowed to take anything to bed after that. Our food was very plain and, because of the war, not very adequate. We were always hungry. I especially remember our usual Saturday dinner: it was bread soaked in gravy followed by a milk pudding. I suppose it could not have been that bad because we thrived alright. Of course, we were never allowed to leave anything on our plates.

I was always weaker than Muriel and Mother had had a job to get me dry at night, although she managed to do this before we came to the school. After a few nights at the orphanage, however, I began to wet the bed again. You can imagine my horror when Nurse found out. She took me to the bathroom and held my head under the cold water tap, then she beat me with my hairbrush. This treatment went on for sometime until, I suppose my body got the message. Unfortunately this treatment left a very bad impression on me all my life, in more ways than one. Whether it was due to my bed wetting I do not know, but Nurse Springthorpe seemed to have a strong dislike for me.

After a time I began to have nightmares and would wake up screaming. Instead of trying to reassure me that it was only a dream, Nurse would get me out of bed and make me stand beside it until I stopped crying. If I went on too long she would stand me behind a large cupboard, this was very frightening as it was pitch dark behind there. Oh, how I longed for my Mother or Moo-moo. This too left a deep impression on me as I have been terrified of the dark all my life.

I used to like lessons because we had a very nice teacher and although she was strict she was fair. I was not a clever scholar, but of course being in the infants' school we learnt the three R's. You can imagine how strict our upbringing was in those days. It was at home, too, but without the cruelty.

One day we were in a long crocodile walking around the school grounds, when the boy I was walking with told me a rhyme. It went as follows: *I had an Auntie Nellie, who had a wooden belly.* I thought it was ever so funny, but when we got back indoors the teacher called us both out and gave us the cane for being rude. This is something I have never forgotten, but it has not dampened my sense of humour.

Every Sunday we had clean pinafores and after dinner we had to line up in the dormitory for nurse to inspect them. If we had a dirty mark on them we would be beaten. One Sunday while we were lined up I wanted to go to the toilet. It is true I had a gravy mark on my pinafore, and I knew I was in for a thrashing, but when I asked Nurse if I could be excused, she refused. When nurse saw the stain on my pinafore she thought I had asked to be excused to get out of the beating. Whilst she was thrashing me I pooh-ed over the floor. In her rage she rubbed my face in it and marched me all round the dormitories, to show the other girls what a filthy little beast I was. Muriel says to this day that she can still see me with my face covered in my own excrement. That was not the end of my punishment, because that night I slept in the bath with just a pillow and blanket for comfort. You cannot imagine how frightening that was for a seven-year old.

We never went home for Easter or Christmas, but things were a lot easier all round. At Easter all the children who had to stay at school, like us, had Easter eggs. I can still see the picture they made, all set out on the windowsills around the playroom. Some of them were huge. The chocolate was rationed out to us, so it behoved you to be good, otherwise you did not get any. Christmas was a very pleasant time for those who did not go home. Easter and Christmas days were the only times in the year when we had eggs for breakfast. On Christmas morning we all had a stocking at the foot of the bed with a toy, some sweets and an orange in it. It was all very exciting. After breakfast nurse would help us open parcels from home. On Christmas afternoon all the children from all parts of the orphanage would gather in the infants' playroom. There would be a huge Christmas tree set up, and one of the masters would be Father Christmas and hand out lovely toys to us all. After a special tea of jelly and cakes we would go to bed. The dining room was beautifully decorated with streamers and balloons.

Mother used to send us occasional parcels, but I am afraid we did not always get them. Our mothers were allowed to visit us on the first Saturday in the month. How we looked forward to those visits! If there was an infection in the school visiting was not allowed. This is when Mother would send us a parcel. One day during a visit Mother asked if we enjoyed the sweets she had sent us. We told her we had not had any. On asking Nurse about this, she said we had been telling lies. Mother did not believe this, so she asked some other mothers if their children had received all their parcels. After some enquiries, it was found that most of them had not received their parcels. An investigation was carried out and we learnt that the nurse in question had been disciplined.

The orphanage was divided into four sections: the nursery - which took children from six months to five years, the infants - from five to eight and then the juniors and seniors. The infants were mixed, except for the dormitories, of course. The juniors and seniors were segregated. We only saw the boys in church or the dining hall. We were not allowed to speak to them.

We were forbidden to kiss one another, not even our own sisters. The school housed six hundred children and we had to stay until we were sixteen, unless of course our Mother married again.

There were three infant girls' dormitories and three for infant boys. On the landing at the top of the stairs, leading to our dormitory was a large cupboard, where our boots were kept. How we hated that cupboard, because one of the favourite punishments of Nurse Springthorpe was to shut us in this cupboard. It did not matter how frightened we were, she would leave us there until she thought we had had enough punishment. The cupboard was full of cobwebs and spiders and I have suffered from arachnophobia ever since.

I hated Sundays in the infants, because Nurse was in charge of us all day. When Nurse Springthorpe was on duty we knew there would be trouble of some kind of other. One Sunday one of the girls did something wrong and when nurse asked who did it no one owned up. Nurse thought she would punish some of us, including me. We had to line up in front of her and she put a towel round our necks. Producing a pair of scissors she pretended to cut our tongues out. You can imagine how terrified we were. We were frightened to tell Mother how we were being treated because we knew Nurse would deny it and we would suffer even more as a result.

The summer of 1918 was very hot, and one day we were playing in the playground when my friend and I wanted a drink. Nurse Springthorpe was on duty and we asked if we could go indoors and get a drink of water. She refused us, so Ursula (my friend) and I found a puddle in the bole of a tree and we drank from it. Somehow or other Nurse found out and when we got back to the dormitory she called Ursula and me to her. We were wondering what we had done, we soon found out. Nurse asked us if we had a drink in the playground, we knew we dare not say no because it was obvious she knew we had. We told her, yes we had drunk from a puddle. I don't think I will ever forget the thrashing she gave us, and for the second time I had to sleep in one bath and Ursula in the other. Not long before this incident, for some unknown reason, I was made Nurse's Prefect. This entailed emptying her teapot and washing her cup and saucer up. One day I accidentally broke her teapot but when I went to tell her, I was told she had gone off duty and would not be back until later. I put the broken pot back in the cupboard but forgot to tell her about it in the morning. Oh dear! That put paid to any more prefecting!

In 1917 our sister Ethel came to the school. She was a real charmer, whatever she did was accepted by all and sundry. The first day she arrived she pinched the girls' bottoms as we were lining up to get into the dining hall. Muriel and I thought it was very brave of her. When nurse asked her what her name was she replied, "Timothy Titus." We thought she would be told off for being cheeky, but, oh no, not Ethel. Nurse thought it was very funny!

Muriel did not get into as much trouble as I did, although one day she turned all the taps on in the washbasins in the bathroom and left them running.

She did get a good hiding for that and she had to spend the day with her hands tied behind her back. As I mentioned before she was not in the same dormitory as me and I think her nurse was more human.

As the reader can imagine I did not enjoy my first years at the orphanage. After the summer holidays of 1918 Muriel and I went to the juniors. Unfortunately during the holidays my friend Ursula died. We also learnt that Nurse Springthorpe had been sacked. What a pity I ever met her!

3

1918-1926

The family in 1919 on the steps of Grandfather Varnham's house in Dalson. Back row from left, Bert, Bill, May. Middle row from left, Phyllis, Muriell. Front row from left, Frank and Ethel (Dick)

When we went to the juniors in the autumn of 1918 we saw very little of Ethel, except once a month when Mother came to visit us. Then we would be together for two hours. This same year Frank, who was then three years old, came to the school. I can picture him being carried by the nursery nurse down the corridor, with we three girls and Mother following. The nurse in charge of the nursery was one of the nicest people at the school.

I thought our life in the juniors would be much nicer than that of the Infants, but I reckoned without the senior girls. In those days fagging was at its worst and we first year juniors were chosen by the seniors to be their fags. We had to clean their shoes and brush their hair and take messages to their friends. If we did not do things right we suffered for it. One of the worst things we had to do for a punishment was to collect as many pins as we could from the girls, who were sewing, and our tormentors would stick them up around our collar. Every time we moved we were pricked, sometimes we had to stand for all our playtime like that. How I dreaded injections when I was older!

The Headmistress in that first year was a dreadful person, she would give us the cane for the slightest thing and she ignored the fagging and bullying that went on. She was called Miss Bateman. In our second year things became a lot happier; we had a new Headmistress, Miss Nixon. She stopped all fagging and bullying and anyone caught doing these things was severely punished. Muriel and I joined the Brownies and later on the Guides. When Mother was able to visit us we were allowed to keep the sweets or whatever she brought us.

Our first year mistress was not very nice, if we got our sums wrong she would thump us hard in the back or in the winter rap us across our knuckles, chilblains and all. You can imagine how painful that was. Muriel and I were now in the same dormitory, so I was much happier.

We had a half-holiday on Wednesdays and Saturdays, this was when the tuck-shop was open. When we were lucky and had some money, which as far as Muriel and I were concerned, wasn't very often, we were allowed to spend sixpence (in today's money, two and a half pence.) The senior boys ran the tuck-shop; that was the only time we were allowed to talk to them.

The junior and senior schools were divided into three houses: Elizabeth, Victoria and Boadicea. I was in Elizabeth, Muriel was in Victoria and when Ethel came up from the infants, she was in Boadicea. We played hockey and netball and went swimming. Each house would compete against each other for the different cups. One year I won the swimming cup for my house, I think it was the only thing I really achieved. Muriel was hockey goalkeeper for her house and I was for mine. Muriel was also goalkeeper for the school team but I played half-back. We also played rounders.

I mentioned earlier that we had a very beautiful chapel. We had to attend twice a day during the week and three times on Sundays, including Sunday School.

In the playground was what we called the 'punny' line, in other words the punishment line. When we had done something wrong, instead of playing games we had to march up and down this line. Sometimes there would be quite a few girls on the punny line, at other times none at all or only one or two. If it was wet during playtime and we were on detention, we had to stay in the classrooms. Lines were the favourite punishment, sometimes we would have 1000 to do. The Headmistress's favourite lines for us to write out were: *"The consequences of your actions are inevitable."* We somehow acquired the art of using three pens at a time. I remember once the whole of our class had to do 200 lines for one of the mistresses. We thought we were being ever so clever when we all decided to do 150. Needless to say, it didn't work, so we had to do them all again, but double the amount.

One day when Mother came to visit us we asked her where Will, Bert and May were. Mother told us the two boys were at another school on the other side of London, but May was going to stay at home and help Grandma and was going to school near by. Sometimes we three girls were allowed to visit Frank in the nursery. When we came up to the Juniors, Muriel and I made friends with a girl called Ruth, she was great fun. Ruth was just a day younger than us.

On May Day we would dance around the Maypole and have a lot of fun. Guy Fawkes' night was something to remember, a huge bonfire would be lit in the boys' playground. There would be fireworks galore, provided by the school committee. Every summer term a fair would come to the school. This was great fun, we were all given sixpence to spend, although the fair people did allow us some free rides.

We used to play lots of games. One was called *Dead Man's Dark Scenery*. This entailed two sides being chosen, it did not matter how many were on a side. First of all, we would get our coats from the cloakroom. One side would then leave the room. Each side had a captain, she would choose who were to be the dead men. These dead men would lie on the floor and the rest of the team would cover them with their coats. The captain then told the others to hide. The captain would then fetch the other team in and they had to guess who were under the coats, in other words who were the dead men. This was one of our favourite games. Another one was "*statues.*" One of the girls would be chosen for the "sculptor" and another two would be the judges. All round the playroom were lockers where we kept our own personal belongings. In "statues" we would stand on the lockers and the "sculptor" would pull us down one by one. She would swing us round or drop us. Whatever position she left us in we had to remain still. The judges would then decide who was the best statue and they would be chosen to be the next sculptor. We also played *"I'm on Tom Tiddler's ground."* One girl would be chosen for Tom Tiddler, the others would stand on the lockers. On the word "go" we would all jump off the lockers singing "I'm on Tom Tiddler's ground, picking up gold and silver," which we would be pretending to pick up. Tom Tiddler had to try and catch one of us, and we would do our best not to be caught. The first one caught would be the next Tom Tiddler; you can guess the noise we made. One day we were playing this game just before going into evening chapel, when running to get back on my locker I fell and split my chin open; off I had to go to the sanatorium to have it dressed.

Every week in the infants we were given a mug of liquorice powder to drink, anything more revolting I have yet to find. It would cling to your mouth for ages. Once we tried to hold it in our mouths so we could spit it out after Nurse had gone; what fools we were to think we would get away with it. In future we had to say, "Thank you, Nurse," so that she knew we had swallowed it. When we went up to the juniors and seniors we used to have syrup-of-figs once a week. I quite liked that, and it was only a spoonful, not a mug.

The chapel was closed during holiday time, so the pupils who did not go home went to a church in the village. We quite enjoyed this because we had to go to the gallery and we could look down on the people in the chancel.

I mentioned before that at Christmas Muriel, Ethel, Frank and I never went home. We had the nicest time that the school could provide for us, as not many of us stayed behind. I remember going to a big party near Liverpool Street Station. There were children from other orphanages as well as our own school. We were all given very nice presents and came back with a parcel of goodies. The reason why we did not go home was not because Mother did not want us, but because there was no room for us all at Grandma and

Grandpa's. Will and Bert went home just for the two days because their school closed for that time.

When we went up to the Seniors life became very much better. During the holidays we were allowed to go to the village on our own. Our favourite place was a little sweet shop. We would stand outside the shop and take the farthings out of our shoes we had saved up and spend them in the shop. It was surprising what you one could buy for one penny.

As soon as we started our periods we were transferred to the top dormitory, this was built over the chapel. Once we got there we were supposed to act like young ladies. I am afraid we thought differently! What fun we used to have. There were four rows of beds, about ten in a row. In three corners of the room were the bedrooms of the three mistresses, the fourth led to the bathroom. We would choose sides and leap frog over the beds, seeing which side got to the end first. We were making so much noise one night that one of the mistresses came out of her cubicle and gave us all lines to do the next day; we did not know she was there. We had to be in bed between eight and nine. Of course it was still very light in the summer time, we were not ready to go to sleep. Another game we used to play was blanket swings. Two girls would stand on one bed and another two on another, facing each other holding a blanket, another girl would get into the blanket and the four girls would swing her backwards and forwards amid shrieks of laughter.

Ruth, Muriel and I were always together, our favourite pastime in the dormitory involved a broom. We would take this out of the maids' cupboard and one of us would carry it, with the other two walking either side and sometimes quite a few other girls following on behind. When we were ready, someone would start making the sound of a drum. We would march round the dormitory holding the broom upright and sing:

> *The drums are muffled, he passeth by,*
> *The gallant lad who is doomed to die.*
> *Oh that the terrible deed was done,*
> *The last pangs over, his rest begun.*
> *The last pangs over, his rest begun.*

On the last word someone would shout "fire", the broom would then be dropped and we would all salute it. Reading this now it all seems very childish, but in those days we had to make our own fun. Some nights we would lie in bed and see who could flick their garters farthest. Sometimes they would land on the beams overhead – the broom came in very handy then! If we could not get them down we would have to rely on our knicker legs to keep our stockings up.

We were told nothing about our periods or why we had them. I know that on the day that I started, I nearly fainted with the pain. The mistress sent me to the nurse who explained nothing about it, just to report to her every month. Mother did send us a book on growing up, but we did not understand it, so we just accepted things as they came. Ignorance was indeed bliss in our case. We never talked about these things between ourselves. One of the girls was so frightened when it first happened to her that she laid in a cold bath for ages thinking the bleeding would stop. She was on holiday at the time, living with an aunt. I suppose she was too frightened to ask questions. We heard about this after we left. Frank told us when he came home for good that the boys were told nothing about maturing either.

One night I could not sleep because I had a bad foot, so one of the mistresses came and read the Bible to me. I suppose she thought it would help to take the pain away. The next day I was carried over to the San (Infirmary) with a poisoned foot. I was there some time. I had told the nurse that I had a nail in my shoe, but she took no notice. When I told this to the Sister in the San she was very cross and said she would have a word with the nurse about it. We liked to go to the San because the nurses were kind to us; we also had nicer food.

I mentioned before about the food we had – well that was during the war. When we went up to the juniors the war had ended or nearly so. The food was a little different. For breakfast and tea we had two rounds of bread and margarine and a mug of unsweetened cocoa. If we had jam or syrup it would be spread without the margarine so that by the time we got to the dining hall the bread was hard where the syrup had soaked in. Dinners were meat of some kind, either minced or sliced beef with greens and potatoes, followed by some type of milk pudding or duff. We often had fig pudding which I, and many more of us, hated but we had to eat it or it was brought back to us at teatime. We used to have rhubarb and sago some times, we called it frogs' spawn and seaweed. I remember one day we saw the maids bringing in great dishes of jam tarts – a great rarity. One girl on seeing this called out in a loud voice, "Coo – jam tarts!" The poor girl was sent out of the dining hall, so no jam tarts for her!

When we first went to the orphanage, we had to sing "Grace" before meals. There was an organ in the dining hall and one of the masters would play it. After some time, instead of singing the grace the master on duty would say it. Of course we were not allowed to sit until grace had been said. The boys' tables were at the entrance to the dining hall so if they were in before the girls they had to stand in their places and wait for us to pass. Sometimes we would 'accidentally' push them as we passed by, knowing they could not retaliate.

At this stage of my story I will introduce you to Mr Rickets, the Engineer. He maintained the boilers and did any repair work necessary. He was one of the kindest men I have ever met. He lived with his large family in a cottage in the grounds of the school. If, as in the case of my foot, anyone had to be carried over to the San, he would do it. During the holidays he taught us to row on the Eagle Pond in the school grounds. He was always there when needed. There was also a carpenter attached to the school, but the boys saw more of him than we did, because he taught them carpentry.

One day we were told that someone very important was coming to school. You can imagine our surprise when the Head told us it was Queen Mary. We were rehearsed on how to curtsy to her. We had to present her with purses of money. I don't know where they came from, but I know we were all very excited and also extremely nervous. I can see her now sitting on a big chair looking very regal. Another time her son, Prince Henry came. Ethel was in the Juniors by then and she was told to open the door for the Prince. How proud Muriel and I felt that our sister has been chosen for such an honour.

When we were in the Seniors the school formed a Festival Choir. This was mixed, boys and girls. Muriel had a very nice singing voice and she was leading choir girl. I was not in the choir because I was told that they did not want two members of the same family in it. One day the Choir went up to the London Palladium and sang in front of the Prince of Wales (the late Duke of Windsor). I was never jealous of Muriel doing these things without me; I think I was more proud of her than anything.

There was a huge wooden fence dividing the girls' side of school from the forest. One hot summer's day the fence caught fire. Coo – what excitement that was! We had to keep right away from it naturally, so we all stood on the fire escape to watch proceedings. One of the girls started to kneel down and pray to God to save the school. We could not understand her because we were a good way from the fire itself, but it did cause a great deal of excitement. After the fire a huge corrugated iron fence was put up, so there was no more risk of fires.

The school was badly affected by the dreadful influenza epidemic after the war. Almost all the children went down with it, as well as most of the staff.

Some of the dormitories were turned into hospital wards as the Sanatorium became full. Unfortunately one of the girls contracted tuberculosis, and she died soon afterwards. She was one of our age group and we missed her very much. One day Ethel was admitted to the San suffering from diphtheria. She was very ill for a long time. Of course we could not visit he because of the risk of infection.

We were very sorry when Miss Nixon left; she was a good headmistress. Our next Head was called Miss Brown. She was more strict than Miss Nixon, but like her predecessor, was very fair.

One day, for some reason, the whole school had to do detention. Instead of going out to play after dinner, we all had to march up and down the playroom. Our dinner that day was some form of pea soup. Unfortunately, as we marched, one girl after another began to feel ill. Many of us were violently sick and several of the girls fainted. The punishment was stopped and after some investigation it was found that we were suffering from food poisoning, as the boys as well as the girls were affected.

In 1920, we all went home for the summer holidays. You can imagine the excitement for us three girls. It was the first time we had seen May, Bert and Will since going to school over four years ago. The boys only stayed for a couple of days because they went to spend the rest of their holidays with a cousin in Torquay. During the holidays Mother took the other five of us to Leigh-on-Sea for a week. We stayed in a holiday home run by some nuns. Frank had to sleep at Aunt Edie's house, which was nearby, because males were not allowed in the convent. I cannot describe the feeling of being with Mother again, if only for a short while. When we came back from the seaside we stayed with Grandma and Grandpa for the rest of the holiday. Grandma was a lovely lady. Mother was working in the Bank of England at the time, as a clerk, therefore we only saw her in the evenings, but I remember we used to take it in turns to sleep with her. During the war Mother had been one of the first women police officers, but when it was over she took up clerical work. One day Grandma asked us to go to the market to buy some plums, of course May knew where it was. We took Frank, the five-year-old, with us. On the way home we ate some of the plums. Frank said he would tell Grandma, so we gave him some to shut him up, so we thought. As soon as we got home Frank told Grandma that the girls had eaten the plums. I thought she was going to be cross with us, but she only said, "Well, I shan't be able to make so much jam."

One Sunday during our holiday, Grandpa took us all over the City. He pointed out the lovely work on the gates leading to different buildings and the wonderful buildings and churches. He loved the City. He knew every inch of it. He died a few months before Hitler ravaged it, which was a relief. It would have broken his heart to see the devastation the bombs wrought. He certainly would not like the glass boxes put up now. We did not see Grandma again after that holiday, as she died before we went home again.

The day came to go back to school and as you can imagine we did not want to go. There was many a tear shed the first night back in the dormitory. It was six years before Muriel, Ethel and I went home again.

We used to be farmed out to other girls' homes, to whoever could take us in. Muriel went to stay with one of the girl's grandmothers in Faversham. This girl had lost both her parents on the *Titanic*. That year Ethel and I with four other girls stayed in a school in Bognor. One of the mistresses was in charge of us, I suppose we had nowhere else to go. Another year Muriel and I went to stay with a girl's grandmother in Deal but we were not very happy there. Ethel went to stay with one of her friends, I don't know where Frank went. Another year Muriel went back to Faversham and I went with her, and we had a very enjoyable holiday. I remember going hop picking and that we were allowed to roam in the countryside.

Every November the Freemasons would hold a service in the chapel. They would have tea in the dining hall, then they would walk in line down the corridor to the chapel. We girls would line up either side of the corridor and if you were lucky enough or pretty enough the men would slip some pennies in your hand. I can see them now walking along with their aprons on.

One of the mistresses was a very nice singer and pianist, and when she was on duty some evenings, we would gather round the piano in the playroom. She would sing and play to us, she taught us some nice songs. I am afraid I have forgotten most of them after all these years, but I do remember how much we enjoyed those evenings.

Once a year during the summer term we would celebrate Founders' Day. This was when the Old Girls and Boys who had left the school came back. They had tea in the dining hall and there was a service in the chapel. This was quite a nice event because we would join them, and of course a lot of questions would be asked. There would be a cricket match between the Old and present-day boys.

As we got older life was more interesting. One of the mistresses was a keen gardener. She made a lovely garden by the side of the chapel and started us older girls on making a garden. We all had a small plot allotted to us and some how or other we managed to get some seeds. I am sure Miss Stone (the mistress in question) must have bought them for us. She was very enthusiastic about it all. We had a competition at the end of the term to see who had the best little plot. We could grow nasturtiums and mustard and cress and lots of annuals.

I mentioned earlier that we were not allowed to talk in the dining room. There was one exception to this – the last Sunday in the Summer Term at teatime. We could strip our gardens of anything eatable, mustard and cress and nasturtium leaves for example and after washing them under the tap, we were allowed to have them with our rounds of bread and margarine. We were also allowed to talk. I think that was one of the rare times when we could have cake for tea. This was known as "chat Sunday". For a long time we just had two slices of bread put on our plates before we went into tea or breakfast, but towards the end of our time, this was altered and at teatime plates were set in the middle of the table with piles of bread on them for us to help ourselves, and we did so! After a time one of the girls had a good idea. We would have some of the bread at tea and then we would hide one or two slices under our pinafores and take it to our classroom and toast over our smoky fire. We were supposed to do our prep or homework directly after tea, while the staff had theirs. The prefect was in charge, but as she was in with the rest of us, she could not say anything. All went well for some time until one day one of the girls dropped some bread while walking along the corridor. We all had to stop there and then. The mistress then told us to lift up our pinafores. Needless to say we all got lines to do and that was the last of our smoky toast – it was fun while it lasted.

Our grandfather used to do a lot for the orphanage in one way or another. One evening he arranged for a minstrel show to perform at the school. This was a real treat. I remember one of the girls went to sleep during it. I was ever so cross. One evening we were entertained by no less a personage than Henry Ainley, the famous (in those days at least) Shakespearean actor.

1924 was the year I won my only school prize. Prize day was a very important day for us, as you can imagine. Our Mothers were allowed to come and I think Grandpa came once or twice. We had prize giving at the end of the summer term. It was held in the girls' playroom. All the school attended, even the nursery children. I won a prize for scripture and general progress. Muriel won more prizes than I did, I expect she paid more attention in class than me. Our prizes were really lovely books, I am glad to say I still have mine.

In 1925 a dreadful thing happened, three of the girls ran away. I remember that day so well, there was a feeling I suppose of excitement, as to what was going to happen to them. We soon found out when they came back. Apparently, they went to the village to one of the girls' aunts, who of course brought them back. They were punished by being sent to Coventry, heaven help any one who spoke to them. Also every night for a week they were thrashed and we had to stand and watch, I suppose to teach us all a lesson. Poor girls, their punishment lasted a whole week, after that they were allowed to mix with us again.

Our last year at school, 1926, was quite an eventful one. I have already said that we did not go home for Easter, perhaps it was as well because this last year Muriel and I contracted mumps very badly. We could not open our mouths to drink and had to fed through a spout. Of course we were in the San, I don't know how many girls got it, because most of them went home.

I must tell you about the Easter concert the girls put on, this was of course before we broke up. The Headmistress wrote a play with some songs in it. Muriel had the main part, I told you she could sing well. How I was looking forward to seeing her in it, alas, stupid me, the day of the concert I answered one of the mistresses back. I was not allowed to go. I always maintain this was the biggest disappointment of my life. All the girls said how well Muriel did her part. I had to stay in the classroom and write 100 lines. Even though I apologised to the mistress in question she would not let me go.

During that last year one of the Governors thought it would be a good idea to teach the older girls ballroom dancing. We did enjoy these evenings. All went well until it was decided to let the senior boys also learn to dance. The first lesson with them was hilarious: we were so shy of one another. Do not forget we had never been allowed to talk to them. Now they were holding hands with us trying to learn how to waltz. The lessons with the boys did not last very long. We were taught the Lancers, the Valeta and most of the lovely old dances. We were taught these things, but nothing to do with domestic work or home management, so essential to girls in those days!

One day all the senior girls and boys were told to gather in the girls' playroom, we had no idea why. Some of the masters and mistresses were also there. Apparently three of the girls had been caught meeting three of the boys in the cellar. It was quite traumatic, although the master who caught them knew their names, the six culprits had to own up to the whole school, or rather the senior school. When we knew what it was all about most of us thought they would be expelled on the spot, no such thing. The boys got the cane on their behinds and the girls on their hands. I think the reason they were not expelled was because they were all leaving at the end of the term, because they would all reach the age of sixteen years.

Towards the end of the summer term we had Sports Day, trying to win cups for our houses. One day I was practising when I had a most dreadful pain in my side. I was taken to the San and then rushed off to the nearest hospital. There the doctor diagnosed appendicitis. After being prepared for the operation the doctor put it off for the night. In the morning it was decided it was not appendicitis at all, but that I had strained a muscle very badly; so I was sent back to school. A fortnight later Muriel was admitted to the same hospital for an operation for a hammer toe; she was in pain for a long time afterwards.

At the beginning of this term a new mistress came on the staff, a Miss Francis. Unfortunately she could not pronounce her 'rs' so instead of saying "Hurry up, hurry up down the corridor" she would say "Huggy up, huggy up down the coggidor!" We though it was ever so funny. We use to mimic her. She did not come back the next term.

The last summer we were at school Muriel and I went home for the holidays. Grandpa had married again so Mother had to leave the house and find somewhere for us all to live. Mother managed to find a flat for the time being. Muriel and I went down to our aunt at Leigh-on-Sea for a week or so. When we came back from Auntie's, Muriel's foot was very sore – she had managed to get sand in it so it took much longer to heal.

One of the weekends we were at home two of Mother's office friends took us to their home. They were lovely ladies. I remember that they took us to our first theatre. We saw *Thark* with Ralph Lynn and Tom Walls and other well-known actors of the day. We hated having to go back to school but we knew it was only for another term. This was the term when I thought I was going to be expelled!

One Sunday evening, the Headmaster was preaching the sermon in church. He seemed to be just rambling on an on, not making any sense at all. There were a lot of sniggers going on beside me, needless to say I was sniggering as well, trying hard not to laugh, when suddenly in a very loud voice the Head almost shouted out, "Will that girl over there stop laughing." He was pointing his finger straight at me. Gosh, I knew I was in for it! When we came out of Chapel the Head was waiting for me with one of the mistresses beside him. I was called out of line and told to go and wait outside the Headmistress's study. I was really frightened. I felt sure it would be immediate expulsion. As it happened the Headmistress was out that evening so I was told to go to bed and I would be reported to her. In the morning I was informed that I was not to go to Chapel until further notice but during the services I had to wait outside the Headmistress's study. This went on for a week then one of the mistresses said, "Didn't I think it time I wrote a letter of apology to Father Ellis, the Headmaster. This I did and somehow Father Ellis received it. The next day the Head Boy arrived at our classroom asking if I could be excused to see the Headmaster. My mouth was in my boots as I followed the boy through the boy's department. The Head received me very warmly in fact. I was told to sit down and make myself comfortable. After a brief lecture the Head told me he did not consider me a naughty girl, just high-spirited. He shook hands with me and said he expected to see me in Chapel that evening. Of course when I got back to my classroom the girls were all agog to know what Father Ellis had said to me!

By now Frank was in the junior school and was also in the choir. I used to look forward to seeing him coming down the aisle looking angelic. Although Ethel was now in the senior school we did not see a lot of her, she had her own friends and Muriel and I had ours. We were in the upper fourth form but Ruth, being a very clever girl, was in the fifth form.

We should have sat for the Oxford Junior exam at Christmas but we left on our sixteenth birthday at the end of November. Our last day at school was very carefree. Although it was very foggy we did play our last hockey match; mind you, we could hardly see one end of the pitch from the other. We had to visit the Headmaster who gave us his blessing and presented us with a bible and prayer book. And so on the twenty-fourth day of November 1926 we said "Goodbye" to our friends and left school. It was many years afterwards that I learnt from Muriel that she had asked the Headmistress if she would be able to give me a reference. The answer was, "Muriel, Phyllis is one of the most honest girls in the school."

After we had all left school we were able to make a lovely home together and we tried hard to make up to Mother the lost years she had to do without us. Will was now an apprentice in an engineering firm and Bert did a lot of odd jobs until he could get into the Merchant Navy. By the time we left school May was established as a secretary in the City of London, where Mother also worked.

My experience at the hands of Nurse Springthorpe and other left me very conscious of other people's feelings. Through my life I have tried, and succeeded I hope, to be sympathetic and understanding of other's problems. I do not think I have every wilfully hurt anyone physically or mentally.

I was once asked if I hated my mother for sending us away. I was quite shocked and replied, "Why should I, she suffered more than we did?"

4

1926-1928

Before we left the orphanage Mother had found a flat for us. On leaving the school we were fitted out with clothes. We were taken to a shop in Leytonstone and were given three sets of underwear, some black stockings, a pair of outdoor shoes, a pair of indoor shoes, a navy coat and hat. This was because we were not going to live at home. Grandfather and our new step-grandmother had decided that we would go into service. That is why we had to have a navy blue hat and coat, it was part of the uniform of under-nursemaids. We spent a week at home after leaving school so that May could make our uniform dresses. We were both full of qualms about the future as we had been given no domestic tuition at all. We were literally being thrown in the deep end.

I was to be nursery maid to the Earl and Countess of Cavan's daughter, Lady Elizabeth Lambert, who was nearly two years old. They lived in a large house in Great Cumberland Place, near Hyde Park. Muriel was to be nursery maid to Captain and Mrs. Wedgwood-Benn's children, Michael, aged four, and Anthony who was eighteen months. So you see, dear reader, we were going to be parted again.

The work was very hard at first. I had to be up at six in the morning to get the day nursery ready. This entailed lighting the fire, black-leading the hearth, sweeping and dusting, all before seven o'clock, when I had to wake Nurse with a cup of tea. That first week was sheer hell. I never thought I would get through all the work, let alone do it properly. Nurse was a real martinet. In the nursery her word was law. Little Elizabeth and I got on really well. She was a real sweetie. She could not say Phyllis so she used to call me "Fishes". There was another daughter in the house, ten-year-old Daphne. She did not come into the nursery very much as she had her own governess, a very nice Scottish lady.

Both Muriel and I were paid seven and sixpence a week, but of course we lived in so it was really only pocket money, for fares home mostly. I was allowed a half-day on Wednesday and every other Sunday off. I rarely got away before three o'clock on Wednesdays because I had to do Miss Daphne's bedroom and wash the schoolroom floor. By the time I got home it was four o'clock and I had to back at the house by ten. The household was a large one and I had to share a bedroom with three other girls. I did not like that because they did not talk to me. We also had to wash in cold water. This I could not understand as we always had hot water in the orphanage.

One day, as I was carrying Nurse's tea tray into the lift, the Earl got in with me. He had a gammy leg, I later learned that he had fallen off his horse while hunting. He should have been on a tour of Australia with the Duke and Duchess of York (later King George the Sixth and Queen Elizabeth, who became the Queen Mother.) Halfway up the lift stopped. I was terrified. The Earl was pressing the lift buttons and shouting for help. We were not trapped for very long but I have avoided travelling in lifts ever since.

Queen Mary was Lady Elizabeth's godmother, and on the child's third birthday she came to visit her. Of course I had to clean the nursery more thoroughly that day. When the Queen arrived I was told to either go to the staff dining room or stop in the night nursery which adjoined the day one. I chose the later venue so that I could peep through the door or keyhole. The visit only lasted a few minutes but my little lady behaved herself very well, and of course the Countess was there too.

One day whilst cleaning Daphne's room, her governess asked me why I was doing this kind of work. She thought I was wasting my schooling. I heartily agreed with her. I really hated the work as the other staff looked down on me because I came from an orphanage. I left the Cavan's at the end of February in 1927.

Muriel's work was much the same as mine, although she did have to clean and polish the baby's pram. I was lucky enough to have one of the male staff do that for me. One day Muriel was told to scrub and whiten the front steps of the house. As she had no idea how to do it she made an awful mess of it. When she told Mother what she had been doing Mother was very angry and wrote to Mrs. Benn saying her daughter was not employed to clean steps and if it happened again she would take Muriel away. Soon after that Captain Benn asked

Muriel if she would like to help him in his parliamentary work. My sister said she was a bit apprehensive at first, but soon enjoyed the work. She was allowed an hour off every day from her normal duties to help him.

The Benn's (later Viscount and Viscountess Stansgate) lived in Grosvenor Road, off Millbank in Westminster. One January night in 1928 the Thames burst its banks and flooded all that area. That night Muriel was sleeping downstairs in the basement where the cook and the other maid slept. Anthony was not very well so nurse told Muriel to take all her belongings downstairs so that Michael could have her room while the baby was ill. Muriel told us later that she woke to a lot of shouting, and wondering what it was all about, she got out of bed and found everything was floating in water. She grabbed her coat, woke the cook and the other maid, then rushed upstairs to wake the family. Fortunately they were all right. She took baby Anthony to safety. Muriel lost everything in the floods but, thank God, she was unharmed. There were others that were not so lucky that night. I will never forget that day. When Muriel did arrive home she had one of Mrs. Benn's dresses on, some underwear of Nurse's and her own coat and shoes. Mother heard about the flood on the wireless so she sent Bill up there to find out what was happening. Bill hung about for a time as the police would not let him through. His relief, when he got home and saw his sister safe, was indescribable. Muriel said she saw her small possessions floating on the gutter. Her knickers were clinging to the railings and a large piece of beef was floating in the lavatory pan. Muriel left the Benn's soon after that and went into clerical work. She became an accounts clerk at the Civil Service Stores in the Strand. In later life the more Conservative members of the family were not sure that they could forgive Muriel for saving the life of someone who was to become such a prominent Socialist!

That year mother managed to acquire a large flat over a chemist's shop, in Queensbridge Road, Dalston. This was the time we really began to live together. Frank was still in the orphanage but, at least, he had a home to come to during the holidays.

I was not out of work for very long. Although I vowed never go back to domestic work, I did. I became house-parlour maid to a Doctor Lewis, near the Middlesex Hospital. She was a brain specialist and a very nice person. The only other member of staff was the housekeeper, Mrs. Harris. She was very kind to me and taught me a lot about housekeeping. The doctor gave a lot of dinner parties and Mrs. Harris showed me the right way to lay the table and also how to serve. I really enjoyed working there, especially as I had my own bedroom. Unfortunately this job only lasted a few months because the doctor became ill and retired to the country. Before we left the doctor asked us to spring clean the flat thoroughly. She had a woman in to do all the heavy work, but she wanted all the cupboards turned out. I remember I opened one cupboard and inside it was a long box and, on opening it, I almost dropped it for inside was a skeleton. I closed the lid sharply and shut the door!

My next job was something entirely different. I became a telephone clerk to a bookmaker. Until that time I had never answered a telephone in my life. I soon picked it up. All I had to do was write down any bets that came through and hand them to the boss, though it was all Greek to me. The poor man suffered from rheumatism and used to send me out to the local market to buy watercress for him. Whether this did his rheumatics any good or not I never found out.

It was about this time that I began to have some odd turns. It is difficult to describe them. I would suddenly lose all power to my limbs and collapse. I had to give up work. Mother said sometimes I would shout out, "Leave me alone, I'm sorry". Mother took me to the doctor who could not diagnose the trouble so he made an appointment for mother to take me to see a nerve specialist. The specialist was none other than Sir Farquah Buzzard, who was the specialist to King George V. I can see him now with his bushy eyebrows and moustache. He told mother it was epilepsy and that I would never get better. Poor Mother, I can still see her crying. I was sent away for two months to an epileptic home in Godalming. The doctor there said it wasn't epilepsy but a form of hysteria, which in time would improve. When I came home I was given valerian to take, the taste was appalling. After a time they changed it to asafoetida. I had to take this in the garden because the smell was so awful. I used to fall about all over the place, many a time I was taken to the local hospital for falling over in the street. They never found anything wrong with me and, thank God, I grew out of it.

Ethel left school in 1928, but she did not come home. She did one year's training in the school nursery, she really wanted to be a proper nanny. After a year she went to a Nursery Nursing College in Islington, obtained her certificate and became fully qualified. I mentioned earlier on in the story that when we went to the orphanage we had to have our hair cut short like a boy. When Grandpa first saw her he said "This isn't our Ethel, we will have to call her Dick." And "Dick" she was for the rest of her life!

Muriel and I were very shy when the boys brought their friends home. We use to ask mother if we could go out but she insisted we stay in and learn to be sociable. We joined the church choral society with Bill and May. We also joined the social club. How wise Mother was. As I was much better I managed to get a job at Snare's, a children's clothing factory in New North Road, Shoreditch. I enjoyed this work and made many friends. Bill was now working for a successful firm of engineers and Bert was a steward on one of the Orient liners. May was quite happy doing her secretarial work in the city and mother was still working as well.

There were three assistants in the chemist's shop above which we lived, as well as the dispenser and the owner. The three assistants were single. What fun we used to have with them. I went out with one called Jock for a little while, he was the first man to kiss me. I don't think I enjoyed it much as he had a very rough moustache. We weren't together very long. He did not turn up for work one day and, after some inquiries were made it was discovered he had committed suicide. We heard later he had been in financial difficulties. One of the other men was called Norman. He used to tease Muriel something shocking. He said to her one day "Kiss me darling, nothing makes me sick!"

The shop was on a corner and it had a huge window on the staircase which overlooked the road. Opposite to us was Brooker's, a gentlemen's outfitters. They also had a large window on the stairs looking into ours. One day I was carrying the chamber pot up the stairs and I looked out of the window, and there staring across from the other side of the road was one of the men from the gent's shop. He had the cheek to wave to me. I think I blushed scarlet and ran upstairs. I later learnt that his name was Ralph and he had been trying for weeks to attract my attention. He was the man I was to marry, but that comes much later.

Bill was courting a very nice young lady called Dorrie. She belonged to the church social club that we had joined and was also in the choral society. We all used to go dancing at the Hackney or Shoreditch Town Halls. May was a lovely dressmaker. Some Sundays we would go with mother to Petticoat Lane market and buy material for our dance dresses. I can remember our first ones. They were made of taffeta, Muriel's was mauve and mine was pink. May made little evening bags out of the same material, they were very pretty.

One day when Dick was training in Islington she was taken ill. She was going to come home for the weekend so she asked one of her friends, also a trainee, to call home and let mother know. Frank was home when she arrived and he told us after that he had never seen such a plain looking girl before. The next time Dick came home she brought her friend with her. She was called Nancy. It is true she was very plain looking but she was full of fun. One had to be if you were with Dick. Frank did not have much to say to Nancy then, but in a few weeks time he came to realise that beauty can be skin deep. Yes, you've guessed it, reader, they eventually fell in love and were married.

On our eighteenth birthday mother and May took Muriel and me to the opera. What a treat that was. We saw *Pagliacci* and *Cavalleria Rusticana*. I felt I was in fairy land, the excitement and wonderment of it all. I really cannot describe how I felt, and I know Muriel was sharing the same feelings as myself. I will never forget the thrill of that evening at Sadlers Wells theatre. This was our introduction to the opera, we went several times afterwards with our boyfriends.

1930-1935

Bill and Dorrie were married on August 23rd 1930. Unfortunately May was suffering from flu. She did her job as bridesmaid very well but was back in bed immediately after the reception. Isn't it funny how things like that stick in ones mind? We had a lot of fun helping Bill transport his personal belongings to his new home in Kingsbury NW9. I remember the day we took his trouser press over, on the Underground, it wasn't the easiest of things to carry on an escalator. We managed it somehow and had a lot of fun doing so.

We had a very large lounge in our home over the chemists shop and on May's 21st birthday Mother gave her a lovely party. All the staff from the chemist shop were invited including the owner, his wife and their family. We had games and dancing and a good time was had by all. Before the owner went home he went to check all was well in his shop. He returned very quickly and asked two of his men to give him a hand downstairs. Apparently a large bottle of olive oil had broken, spilling its contents all over the floor. You can imagine the mess. The owner took it in good part and I think mother was glad she had invited him to the party.

It was about this time that Muriel and I started to go to night school to learn shorthand and typing. I got on all right with the typing but could not pick up shorthand very well. Muriel was the same. On November 24th 1931 Muriel and I became of age -

21 in those days. Again Mother came up trumps and gave us a party, not over the shop this time, but in a hall nearby. I did not know Ralph very well at that time so he wasn't asked to come. He told me years later he was ever so disappointed not to have been invited.

1932 was a memorable year as Ralph and I began to see more of each other. I remember the first time he took me out to the pictures. We saw Ben Lyon in Hell's Angels, not a very romantic film. It was some time before we kissed one another, I was still rather shy of men. One night I was kissing him goodbye when I happened to look up. May and Muriel were watching. I think Mother told them not to be spoilsports!

When Bert came home on leave in the Spring of 1932 he put a proposition to us all. He said he had been doing a lot of thinking and thought first of all it was time for Mother to give up work and, secondly, he would put the deposit down on a house, if we, between us, could afford to pay the monthly mortgage. We were thrilled at the idea of having a house all to ourselves. Bert said we could choose where we wanted to live. He said it would be cheaper for us to pay a mortgage than rent. It would be Bert's house when he married, and we could have it decorated to our liking. We chose a house in Coolgardie Avenue, Higham's Park near Chingford. May was earning good wages so she paid the mortgage and with Mother's widow's pension and Muriel's and my wages we managed quite well. It was lovely coming home from work and finding Mother at home.

'Stromboli' Coolgardie Avenue, Higham Park, the family home in 1932

We moved into the house in October. It was a large corner house with four bedrooms, a very large lounge, dining room, a lovely fitted kitchen, and a good sized garden back and front. I was loath to be moving so far from Ralph, but we still were able to see each other twice a week, on Thursday evenings and on Sundays. These next few years were some of the happiest of my life. Bert called the house 'Stromboli', as he said with so many women living together there was bound to be the occasional eruption. He was wrong. I cannot remember any of us quarrelling.

Frank left school in 1931. He followed our father's footsteps into law. I remember him telling us that at his first interview for the job the man interviewing him asked him if his father's name was William Ernest. Frank told him it was and the man told him he knew Father well as he used to work for him. Frank was delighted to know that and so was Mother.

Bert used to come home on leave every three months. He would put a large sum of money on the mortgage to make it lighter for May, so it was paid off very quickly. All the neighbours knew when Bert was coming home because we would put the red carpet out and hang a flag over the front door and we always gave him a large party. We would invite all our friends and Bill and Dorrie would come. Dick nearly always managed to get time off. Sometimes we had as many as forty people in the house. Mother used to warn the neighbours, but most of them said they loved to hear the laughter coming from our direction.

In the Spring of 1933 Ralph and I got engaged. We held a small party at our house. Ralph's family came, his mother, Minnie Ing, two brothers, George and Ron, and his sister, Win. His mother was a widow like ours. Her husband died in 1925 from gas poisoning he contracted in the First World War. They lived in the lower part of a house in Lower Clapton, East London.

After digging the pond at Stromboli in 1933
Back row from left- Ralph, Bert, May, Dick, George Ing, Bill
Front row from left Phyllis, Dorrie, Mother, Muriel

We had a large garden and one day, we all sat down and discussed what we would like to do with it. We all decided that we would like a pond to start with. So, one Sunday Bill and Dorrie came over and Ralph brought his elder brother, George. Bert was also on shore leave so, with Frank, there were five strong men. They took it in turn to dig out the earth. It was very heavy clay so they puddled it which made it look more natural. When it was finished it looked lovely, it was a real feature. We all put something towards the cost of the plants and fish and we all got a lot of pleasure from it. After this George and Muriel went out for a time. Their courtship did not last very long, I wasn't sorry and neither was she.

One day Bert wrote to say his ship was bringing the Australian cricket team over to meet our team to play for the Ashes so Mother made a huge square cake and decorated it like a cricket pitch. She managed to find some miniature cricketers from somewhere to decorate the cake with. It was a huge success. We had our usual big party and, after tea we played sardines. A couple of Mother's friends came, he was a huge man and his wife a little dot, they were a lovely couple. Doug, the very large man, picked the straw to be the first sardine. He went to hide and after five minutes we others had to start looking for him. He chose Mother's bed to hide on. Dear reader can you imagine about twenty of us on a single bed with a twenty stone man underneath? I can see us all, one big laughing mass of humanity. Before Mother could go to bed that night the boys had to take her bedsprings off and, laying them on the lawn put the roller over them! Another time we played 'Murders'. I have never yet found out how Muriel and Ralph got their behinds wet. They said they fell in the bath and there was some water in the bottom.

On fine Sundays a crowd of us, anything between twenty and thirty, would meet outside Chingford Station and have a picnic in the Forest. We would play ball games and have a lovely time. If it was wet everyone would congregate at our house and we would picnic on the sitting room floor. They were lovely carefree days. If there were only a few of us, say about eight, we would play cards, usually 'Pit'. This is about the noisiest card game I know. I can't remember all the rules of the game but I know it was to do with Bulls and Bears at the Stock Exchange. When you wanted a card you shouted across the table to bid. When you had got a set you shouted out "Pit", if you had any breath left! Mother always made two large jugs of drink and we were all provided with a straw. After each game we took it in turns to drink. Mother was a great sport, she joined in all our games.

We girls looked up to Bill and anything he asked us to do we did willingly, even when he asked Muriel and me to go to the ironmonger's to ask for a pound of round holes! He was a terrible tease, so was Frank. One very hot night I decided to sleep in the nude. Before I got into bed I asked Muriel if Frank had come upstairs, she told me she felt sure he had. Wanting to go to the toilet I dashed across the landing to the loo. Unfortunately for me Frank had not gone to bed he was just coming up the stairs that happened to be facing the toilet. He gave one huge guffaw as I literally flew into the toilet locking the door. I thought that was the end of the incident but, oh no, as I started to come out I saw Frank sitting on a large tin trunk which always stood on the landing almost opposite the loo. I dashed back in and shouted for him to go away. His reply was "I am only waiting for you to come out because I want to go too." In the end the girls came out of their rooms to see what was happening. Of course there was a lot of laughter and after a while Mother persuaded Frank to go to his room. He really was a devil. No one thought to bring me a nightie to put on.

On Saturdays Mother and we three girls would often take the bus into Walthamstow to look round the market, we never had much money to spend. One day as I stood up to get off the bus it gave a sudden jerk. Putting out my hand to catch the rail I missed it and accidentally knocked a woman's hat off. Unfortunately for the lady I not only knocked her hat off but also her wig. With great presence of mind I grabbed the hat from her lap and quickly put it back on her head. Oh dear, I put the thing on back to front. I can see the poor thing with her wig and hat all askew. How we got off that bus I can never say. We all laughed but the poor dear was far from amused, although I did apologise profusely.

In 1933 Dorrie presented Bill with a son, Derek. He was a lovely baby. Mother was thrilled to bits to be a grandmother.

There was always a lot more fun when Dick came home. One day she decided to teach Mother how to ride a bike. You never saw anything so funny in your life. There was Mother perched up on the bike with us four girls trying to guide it. Mother had no idea how to pedal and even the neighbours saw the funny side of it. Mind you I can't say too much as I never mastered the art of cycling, neither did Mother. Both May and Muriel had bicycles and they would go for some lovely rides along the country lanes in Epping Forest.

In 1935 May left her secretarial job and became a partner to a friend who owned a poultry farm in Bourne, just outside Cambridge.

Often Frank, Muriel and I would travel up to the city by train. I would get out at Hackney Downs and walk through to New North Road, Shoreditch where my work was, a matter of three miles each way. I was earning 19/6 a week. My fares were 10 shillings weekly return, so that did not leave me much money to play with. I gave my mother five shillings towards my keep. By the time I married in 1936 I was earning 27 shillings a week. The other girls, of course, earned more than I did. They had to travel up to Liverpool Street. Sometimes they would meet Frank on the train coming home. My hours were 9 to 6 weekdays and 9 to 1 on Saturdays. We had three-quarters of an hour lunch break and twenty minutes tea break. That was the only time I sat down. I worked in the packing department, so I was on my feet all day.

I remember Muriel telling me one day when she met up with Frank at Liverpool Street Station they got into a carriage where there was just one very stern looking lady. When they came to an unlit tunnel Frank began tickling Muriel and she kept telling him to stop. When they came into the light again Muriel said the scandalous look on the lady's face was so funny they could not stop laughing. Little did the dear old soul know they were brother and sister having a lark

6

1936-1940

1936 was a memorable year for me. In August Ralph and I spent our first holiday together. We went to a lovely little village called Steyning in Sussex. We stayed with a very nice family. Of course we had separate rooms, no sharing in those days. It was a wonderful holiday. We would walk for miles. The lady of the house packed us up a lunch box each day and we would go home in the evening to a sumptuous meal. We paid twenty-five shillings each for the week.

In September May and Myhill, her partner, came to Ralph and me with a proposition. They wanted a handyman on the farm, being girls there were things too big or to heavy for them to tackle. So they wondered if Ralph would take on the job and if we got married I could help around the farm or in the house. They preferred to have a married couple. We would get a percentage of the profits for our wages. At the time the farm was doing very well. After a lot of serious thought and consultations with both families we decided to accept the job. Ralph's mother was the only real objector. I later learnt she would object to any thing if it meant she would lose her Ralph.

Phyllis and Ralph on their wedding day, December 26th 1936

It was decided that we should start in the beginning of the New Year so we fixed our Wedding Day for

December 26th. The next few months were quite hectic with all the arrangements to be made. I had four bridesmaids: my three sisters and Ralph's sister Win. One Saturday we all trooped up to the West End. In those days there was a guinea shop in Oxford Street, or somewhere around that area. Everything in that shop was a guinea, my wedding dress and the four bridesmaids dresses. They were just as lovely as the ones girls pay hundreds of pounds for today. The bridesmaids were in taffeta, Muriel was in pale blue, May's was deep purple, Dick's a pale mauve and Win's dress was lemon. They carried bunches of anemones. My dress was white satin. The head-dresses were 2/6 from Bourne and Hollingsworth, and their shoes were dyed to match their dresses. I wish I could have had a coloured photo of them, they looked lovely. Their whole outfit cost under two pounds each. Mine was not much more.

It was a foggy day on Boxing Day 1936 but all the thirty guests managed to arrive on time. The wonderful part of that day was the fact that our father's old friend, who was a vicar at a church in East London, took the service for us. The reception was held at home. Bill and Dorrie lent us their house for a few days honeymoon while they stayed with Mother at Highams Park.

On January 1st 1937 we started our new life in Easting Down, Bourne. The farm was a smallholding consisting of eight acres of land. When we started there were only chickens, goats, some geese and ducks. The girls also grew their own fruit and vegetables. As you can imagine there was plenty of work for us all. We all lived in a bungalow. Myhill and her old blind grandfather were living there as well. The cooking and heating was done with an oil-fired Rayburn. Once a week Myhill and May would go to London with eggs to sell. They also took any available fruit and vegetables.

Ralph built a huge barn for storage and as a cow shed. Myhill decided that we could do with a cow to save buying milk from the local farmer. Up to now they had used a lot of goat's milk. When Ralph and I arrived one of the nannies was already in kid. They were pure white goats and not as easy to milk as one would think. We got it down to a fine art in the end. The cow the girls eventually purchased was a little black Dexter, a wonderful milker but a very bad tempered animal. I remember it was a very cold winter that year, we used to wrap up like mummies to keep out the cold when we went round shutting up the birds for the night.

At the beginning of March I began to feel very wheezy at night time. I could not understand what was wrong, until one weekend Ralph and I went up to London to see our families and his mother suggested that I might be pregnant. I did not realise it could be this until I realised I had not had a period for a couple of months, but I put that down to the new life I was leading. How ignorant I was. When it was finally confirmed by a gynaecologist Ralph was not pleased. When we told May and Myhill they made me rest in the afternoon.

The next time the girls went up to London I was picking some flowers in the garden when Ralph came out with a shotgun in his hand. I asked him what he was doing with it. He suddenly seemed to go bezerk, he shouted at me to tell him who was the father of the child I was carrying. He pointed the gun at me and said if I did not tell him he would shoot me. I could not believe my ears. There was this man who I had married only a few weeks ago saying he was going to kill me. I tried to keep as calm as possible and asked him what on earth he was talking about. Then it all came out. His mother told him the child could not possibly be his because we had not been married long enough for me to be carrying his baby. Dear reader, I cannot possibly describe my feelings. There was this man, whom I adored, accusing me of carrying another man's child because his mother said so. I don't know what would have happened if Myhill's grandfather had not come to the door and asked if anything was wrong as he had heard raised voices. In as calm a voice as I could manage I told him it was all right nothing was wrong. Ralph then went back indoors and I ran to the far end of the field and gave way to a flood of tears. I had seen Ralph's mother in a temper over nothing, she was like a screaming witch. I had never seen anything like it, but it never occurred to me it might be a family trait, which unfortunately it was. To me this was something entirely different. It was obvious that Ralph had a lot more faith in his mother and he took her word against mine. I stayed in the field for a very long time as I didn't know what to do, I was very frightened. Its true we were not planning to have a little one so soon but it had happened. May and Myhill had accepted the fact, and for myself I knew there could never have been any one else but Ralph. We had been courting for three years before we were married and our first night was the first time we had intercourse. These thoughts were going through my head as I lay sobbing on the grass. I finally plucked up courage and went indoors. Ralph was busy getting Grandfather's tea. I noticed the gun was back in its place but I never found out if it was loaded or not. Ralph never apologised for upsetting me and I tried to be as normal as possible.

When we went to bed that night Ralph gave me some tablets to take. On asking what they were for he said his mother gave them to him for me to take. When I read the label it said something about abortion. I was furious. I told him I had no intention of killing our child. He started shouting again so I threatened I would tell May what he wanted me to do. He never mentioned it again.

After the third month I used to go to London for monthly check ups. I was going to have the baby in the Salvation Army Mothers' Hospital in Clapton. I was going to have to stay in hospital for two weeks after the baby was born, at a cost of five pounds a week. We paid so much each time we came up. We travelled about in a motorbike and sidecar. My own family were pleased about the baby, especially Muriel.

By this time Muriel was courting, his name was John and he worked in the gentlemen's department of the Civil Service Stores. After a time he lodged with mother and Muriel until they got married.

The last week in August I went for my check-up and the hospital advised me to come up again and stay in London as they did not like the idea of me travelling backwards and forwards in a sidecar when the baby was so near. They told me it would be another three weeks until the baby was born but they wanted to play it safe. On the morning of September the first I woke up feeling strange. I told Ralph I kept wanting to go to the toilet. I thought I must have caught a cold. May and Myhill decided I ought to go to the hospital. When we passed near his mothers street Ralph suggested we call in for a cup of tea. I said no, that we had better carry on. I was not feeling very comfortable. I told him I expected they would give me something for my cold. You can imagine my astonishment on reaching the hospital after telling the nurse I thought I had a cold, when she informed me the baby was on its way. I remember replying that they had told me on Monday that the baby was not due for another three weeks. Anyway, at one o'clock in the afternoon on the first of September 1937 our son Bruce was born. He was just over six pounds in weight. He was known in the hospital as the motorbike baby.

I learned later that the exact time I was having Bruce, Muriel cut her hand very badly. She had no idea I was in labour.

Although I was 27 I was still very innocent, so much so that after Bruce was born I asked my mother if I was still a virgin. She gave me a lovely smile and with a shake of her head and said, "I don't think so, dear."

Bruce was a good baby. If we had to work away from the house I would leave him in his pram with the two dogs, May's Pointer, Don Patches and Myhill's little Scottie, called Grubby. They would keep guard over him, they were wonderful. For the first few months things went quite well, but Ralph's mother kept asking him to come back to London. I did not want to go.

Muriel was married to John on Easter Monday 1938. It was a very sunny but windy day. Once again Father's friend performed the ceremony. Bert was able to come home for Muriel's wedding, he was at sea for mine. Bert also got married that year, in December, to a widow he had met on one of his trips to Australia. Her name was Dorothy. Not many of us knew they were getting married but it meant that Bert needed his house. We had known that he would want it when he got married and that we would have to leave. Anyway for a time Mother went to the farm and I'm sure she was a great help to the girls.

In June of the same year Ralph decided to go back to London. His old boss had written to him saying that they needed him. It was true we had not had much money since coming to the farm so, much against the grain as far as I was concerned, we left Bourne and went to live in Clapton. Ralph's mother had found us a flat. It was in Chatsworth Road, a market street, and was on the top floor over a draper's shop. We had to give up the motorbike as it belonged to Myhill so Ralph bought himself a bicycle to get to and from work. I liked being on our own, but I did not like the new environment. I missed the farm fields and the open air, so I used to take Bruce round Hackney Marshes in his pram.

We soon discovered that the flat was mouse-infected, it was dreadful. I had to be careful about food. I remember one night we caught nine mice. The sooner we emptied one trap and left it to go to bed another would go off. I hated it. I know we were only paying ten shillings a week for the flat but I was terrified in case they got into the baby's cot, which they occasionally did! We complained to the landlord but he said "What do you expect, living over a market?"

Muriel and John were buying their own house in Kenton in Middlesex, not very far from Bill and Dorrie. It was a lovely house with quite a large garden. We did not see very much of each other partly because Ralph could not afford the fares and also because he only had Sundays off. These he spent with his mother. It was about this time I began to realise the hold his mother had over him. When war was declared in September 1939 the people who lived next door to Ralph's mother decided to move to the country and they asked my mother-in-law if she thought Ralph would like to rent the house. He jumped at the idea, any thing was better that our mouse-ridden flat. We moved in

October. At the time I suppose it was a good idea as no one knew what was going to happen.
Muriel's John was called up immediately. He was in the Royal Observer Corps (barrage balloons and all that) so John packed her off to the farm as *she* was now pregnant. The baby was due in December but like me she was going to have it in London. As it happened she stayed with Bill and Dorrie to have the baby. Her son, Anthony David, was born on December 12. I did not know she was in labour but all that day I was doubled up in pain. She did not have as easy a time of it as I did. After two weeks she went back to the farm and Tony was christened in the same little church in Bourne as Bruce had been.

Bill was exempt from National Service because he was working as an engineer making medical instruments. May, of course, was working on the farm and was also exempt. Frank joined the Air Force in 1940 and Bert's ship was commandeered by the navy to escort troops and cargo ships. The family Dick was nanny to moved from London to Berkshire, somewhere near Windsor. After a time she left the family and took up nursing in Windsor Hospital. George, Ralph's elder brother, was first to be called up in his family, he too joined the Air Force. Ron, his younger brother, was next, he joined the army and went into the Royal Electrical and Mechanical Engineers. George married Gertie, the girl who lived opposite his mother's house, in December 1939, and they moved to Hounslow. Frank lived on his own in a flat until 1940 when he married Nan, who had joined the ATS just before they were married.

7

1940-1962

Phyllis and Bruce in 1943

I saw very little of my family for a time. Mother and Muriel stayed at the farm for a while. Then Muriel moved to Ainsdale to be with *her* mother-in-law as John thought they would be safer there, and Mother went to look after Dick and a friend who were sharing a flat in Windsor, opposite the Castle.

Ralph was called up in 1941, he joined the Royal Army Service Corps and, in June, he was sent overseas and spent the next four years and three months in the Middle East Forces Headquarters in Cairo.

In December of that year I got a job as a telegraphist in the Central Telegraph Office in the city. My mother-in-law looked after Bruce while I was working. I was loath to leave him. I refused to allow him to be evacuated out of London, after my childhood experiences I wanted to make sure he was being well looked after.

One day Mother wrote and said Muriel was coming down for the weekend and could I manage to come too? It was OK by my mother-in-law as Win was still at home waiting for her call-up papers. Before going to Windsor I decided to buy a new hat. It was a lovely olive-green velour. I arrived at Windsor soon after Muriel and when Mother opened the door she burst out laughing. It appeared that Muriel had had the same idea about a hat and yes, you've guessed it, it was exactly the same as mine. We all had a good laugh.

Dick got married in 1941 to Ted, a local carpenter. He was a really decent man, very quiet, so different to our sister, but they were very much in love. It was a lovely wedding in spite of the war restrictions. They had a nice flat by the river Thames. Mother got a job in a day nursery after Dick got married.

Before Ralph was called up he turned part of his mother's cellar into an air-raid shelter. He fixed up some beds and made it as comfortable as possible. The lady who lived in the flat above, Mrs Poppy Clayton, slept on a camp bed.

When Bruce was about four years old he got Impetigo, poor little lad. I think this is one of the worst of childrens' complaints. We had to smother his face with ointment at night then cover it with a gauze mask. In the morning we had to take the mask off. Poor child, he used to scream with pain.

One day I took Bruce down to Windsor as Mother said the Queen (later the Queen Mother) was going to visit the nursery. We got a place just by the door, and, as the Queen came out Bruce was swinging his teddy bear around. I just managed to grab his hand but he just hit the Queen's tummy with it. What lovely smile she gave him.

I enjoyed my work at the Central Telegraph Office, although the hours were different each week I was able to get home most nights. Ralph's sister Win was called up in 1943. She joined the WAAF, in the Catering Corps.

Also in this year Dick presented Ted with a son, Frank. I only saw him once as a baby and what a lovely child he was.

In November of that year Bruce was taken very ill with pneumonia. I was frantic. I asked the doctor if it was any good me trying to contact his father. When I told him he was in Egypt he said by the time he got here it would either be to late or the child would be well on the way to recovery. You can guess how I felt. However the doctor said he would try a new drug called M and B. I had to get time off from work to look after him, I could not leave him with my mother-in-law. That afternoon George came home to see his mother and said he would stay the night so we could get some sleep. He said he would call us if there was any change in Bruce's condition. God was good and we both slept soundly, in the morning George woke us with a cup of tea and said Bruce was a lot better.

As children we never went to a pantomime but the following January I took Bruce to see Cinderella. I think I was as excited as the child. On the Monday following the pantomime I received a letter from Muriel saying she had taken Tony to see Cinderella at exactly the same time as I had taken Bruce. So although we were miles apart we were enjoying our first pantomime with our children at the same time. Three weeks before Easter 1944 I took Bruce to the cinema to see a cowboy film with Roy Rogers. He was very concerned about the horses. The next day Bruce developed Scarlet Fever and was taken to an isolation hospital in Tottenham, about five miles away. During his time there Ron came home on leave. I said I was very worried as to how Bruce was getting on as we only got very cursory reports from the hospital. Ron said "Don't worry I'll get in to see him." I told him I was not allowed to, so how on earth was he going to manage it? He did go, and told the Sister he was Bruce's father home from the front line. (It is true that Ron had come from the battlefront, in France.) After donning a gown and mask he followed the Sister into the ward. Ron told us afterwards that he was willing the boy to keep quiet but as soon as he saw Ron he called out, "Oh! Uncle Ron, have you come to take me home?" Ron said he told the sister that Bruce's dad was in Egypt. The sister was very sympathetic and said, "Kids always let you down." I did appreciate Ron's visit.

The day after Bruce came home from hospital he came out in spots - he had the measles. He had had mumps while in hospital! That was a dreadful year for the boy. After measles he got whooping cough, followed by chickenpox and a few weeks later he got German measles. I was backwards and forwards to his school apologising for his absence. His teacher told me not to worry, he would soon pick up where he left off.

Ralph sent us some lovely things from Egypt, such as brooches and jewellery of all kinds, also some very nice cotton underwear for Bruce. This was most welcome as it helped our clothing coupons out.

In 1945 the Channel Islands were liberated. I was still working as a telegraphist at the Central Telegraph Office and I had the honour, at least I still consider it an honour, to open up the communication channel to Jersey, another colleague was doing the same for Guernsey. It really was thrill when the Jersey operator came through and really very emotional for us all, especially as we had to send a message to the people of the islands from the King.

In August there was great rejoicing in our house. Ralph came home. When he left Bruce was a little three-year-old. He came back to find a very intelligent boy of eight years. It was lovely having Ralph back in England and, after two weeks leave, he was posted to Northallerton in Yorkshire until his discharge in February 1946. I gave up working at the telegraph office for a time as Ralph and Bruce were finding it hard to adjust to one another. Unfortunately this was the case with quite a few families where the father had been away for such a long time.

This was supposed to be a story about all my family, but during the war years I did not see very much of them. When John was demobbed Muriel and Tony came back to the house in Kenton. I was ever so pleased because I was able to see more of them. She was also able to visit Bill and Dorrie more. Bert by now had a son and daughter, Christopher and Geraldine. Frank and Nan had set up home in north London, they were never to be blest with children. Mother was still living in Windsor but she had given up the flat and was now living with Dick and Ted. It was there she celebrated her 70th birthday. Dick and Ted put on a great party for her and invited all the family. It was about this

Mother's 70th birthday at Winsor in 1952
Back row from left Dorrie, May, Bill, Nan, Muriel, Bruce, Dick, Derek
Front row from left Phyllis, Mother, Aunt Edie, young Frank, Ted, and
Primrose the Pointer in front on the grass.

time I began to realise just how selfish my mother-in-law was. Naturally I wanted to go to Mother's party and take Bruce with me. Mrs Ing kicked up an awful fuss about our leaving Ralph on a Sunday. He did not want to go. I almost had to plead with him to let me go with Bruce. I went in the end and Bruce was a great comfort to me.

When Muriel and her family returned to Kenton after the war she took on a job as a 'lollipop lady' at a very busy road crossing. One day, soon after being provided with a smart new uniform, she got on her bike and rode to work. As she was getting on her bike after duty she looked down and to her horror saw she was still wearing her bright blue slippers with bobbles on. Muriel said she was surprised no one noticed or told her about it, especially the children. Muriel did this job for nineteen years. She told us that when she came on duty one day a policeman was standing by the crossing holding a little girls hand. He told Muriel the child had told him she was not allowed to cross the road unless the nice lady was there.

1947 was another milestone in our lives. Bert and Dorothy decided to live in Australia. Dorothy was Australian and she wanted to go home. Her mother was there and she had been ill so they thought it best for them to go. We were upset at the time, but it was their life. A few days before they left Bill arranged for just the family to have a farewell dinner in the West End. It was a lovely evening with just us seven children and Mother. Bert and family sailed in March and that was the last most of us saw of them.

This year Bruce sat for the 11-plus exam. He was only nine when he took it. The government wanted to see how the children that had stayed in London during the war had fared against those who had been evacuated. In spite of all Bruce's setbacks he did well. He was offered a place at Christ's Hospital School in Sussex, but I could not bear to send him away. He had been awarded a scholarship so at the age of ten he started at The City of London School for Boys at Blackfriars.

On the 13th September I presented Ralph with a daughter, Beryl Margaret. Again my mother-in-law was wickedly saying that Beryl was not Ralph's daughter, and again, when she found out I was pregnant she had given me some stuff to get rid of the baby. Of course I refused. I really could not understand her, or Ralph. Beryl was to be a great joy to us all.

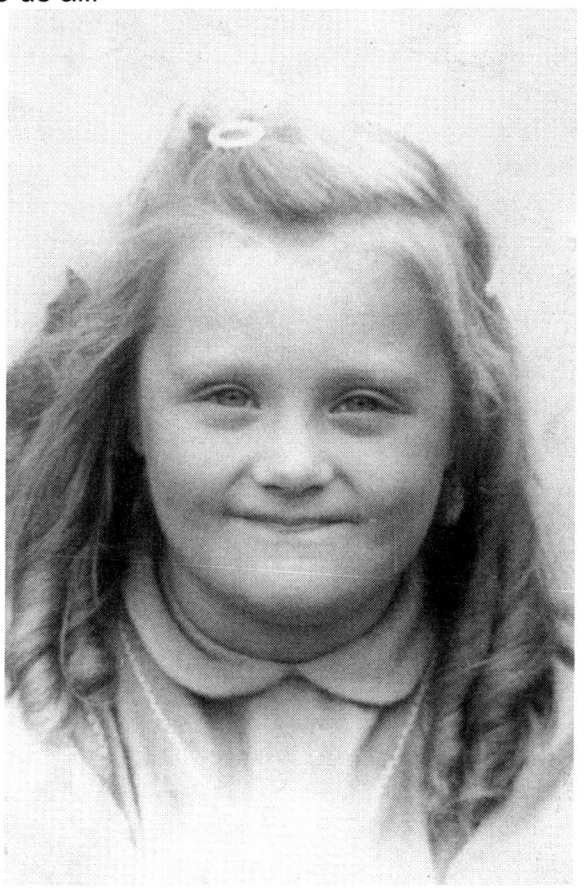

Beryl in 1953

In November of this same year Ron married Pam. Once again mother-in-law tried to make trouble saying she supposed they *had* to get married. What wicked people some women are, especially those who begrudge their sons any happiness.

I was beginning to regret ever moving next door to my in-laws. My life wasn't my own. We were very hard up and although Ralph always managed to find enough money to provide his mother with fruit and titbits, there was never enough for me. I am far from a jealous person but I did use to feel out in the cold. All the Ing family had violent tempers, they had never been taught to control them. I remember I must have crossed Ralph in some way as I remember arguing with him after just giving him a cup of tea, which he threw at me. I dodged and it went all over the new wallpaper he had not long put up. I was laughing to myself inside as I found that really funny.

Two years after their marriage Pam and Ron had a dear little son called Barrie. Unfortunately he was born with a congenital heart condition. He spent most of his life in and out of hospital. Ten years after Dick and Ted's Frank was born they had a daughter called Susan.

When Beryl was a year old I went back to work in the telegraph office. After a few months I was transferred to the Stratford office. This was much better for me, both for working hours and the travelling time, and I made many friends there. Sometimes I was able to work at our local office in Hackney. This was very nice as it was within walking distance from home.

It was about this time that Bill started his own engineering firm. He did very well, as many small companies could at that time and produced standard products for some of the big stores. If he was pushed to get orders out members of the family would help out. I don't suppose he was a very stern taskmaster! Soon after the war May left the farm. Things went seriously wrong between her and Myhill. May was left practically penniless. She had several gardening jobs around the country before finally ending up as a gardener on a farm just outside Bognor. She lived in lovely little Rose Cottage with Mother. Wherever May went she left a lovely garden behind her.

1956 was a sad year for us all. In May Ron and Pam's son, Barrie, died. He had been taken into hospital to have an operation to correct his heart problem but he died on the operating table. He was a great loss as he was such a happy, loveable little boy. In the October fate struck another cruel blow to our family. Dick and Ted's Frank was killed in a road accident. He was coming home from school on his bike when a lorry crashed into him. Thank God he did not suffer. He was only thirteen. He would probably have gone to university as he was a clever boy. It was a dreadful shock to us all. Susan, his sister, was three years old at the time.

The following year Mother developed breast cancer. She had a major operation in Chichester Hospital. She made very little fuss over it and in time made a good recovery. Mother was a widow for nearly fifty years. She told us once that she had had an offer of marriage but when the gentleman found out she had seven children he thought better of it. How we used to tease her about this when we were living together.

This year Win got married, accompanied again with great unkindness from her mother. Ralph had been working as a bus conductor for some time now as the doctor told him to get an outdoor job. He had a very bad chest, mostly because he was a heavy smoker. It was on the buses that he met John, Win's future husband. John was a very quiet man, divorced from his first wife who had his two children. Apparently he came home from work on day to find an empty house except for the minimum of furniture. Ralph took pity on him and one day brought him home for a meal. The next thing we knew was that he and Win were getting married. I have never seen a woman in such a rage as on the day Win showed her mother her engagement ring. She was really wicked to her own daughter instead of being pleased she had found a partner. After all Win was nearly 40! They had a room in her mother's house, but unfortunately for Win her marriage only lasted just over two years as John died of TB in 1957.

By now Bruce had done his two years National Service and had become an undergraduate at St. Johns College, Cambridge. How proud I was. I think his dad was too, but he never showed it. During his vacation he would find a job to help boost his money. Christmas time he would help out at the local sorting office. This was quite a well paid job at the time. During the long summer vacation he was a transport clerk at the local ambulance station. When he was 21 we gave him a lovely party, all my family came and so did one or two of his college friends. This year Beryl sat for the 11-plus exam and went to the local John Howard Grammar School for Girls and did very well there.

In the December of that year (1958) Derek, Bill and Dorrie's son, got married to Gina, whom we all liked very much indeed. I did not see a great deal of my family because when they did visit me they had to go and spend time next door with my in-laws. They did not like having to do this so they did not come very often. I didn't blame them. I went to visit them when I could.

In 1960 Bruce graduated and Ralph and I were so happy to be in the Senate House to see him and his friends. For once Ralph admitted that he was proud of his son. Bruce started to work for the Council for Nature in Kensington and it was good to have him living at home.

After Ron and Pam's Barrie died, Pam had a number of miscarriages and the doctors told her she must not have any more pregnancies. So in 1960 they adopted a six-month-old boy. They called him Adrian. My mother-in-law was not very pleased but Ron told her quietly that it was *their* business. Two years later they adopted a two-month-old girl whom they called Julia.

8

1962-1964

In 1962 Win said she wanted to go back to work, so it was decided, by my in-laws, that I should stay at home and look after my mother-in-law and Beryl. Ralph said we would be able to manage. I loved being at home looking after Beryl but I was supposed to spend most of my time next door. I found myself hating my mother-in-law more and more. She told tales to Ralph about me. She said I could not keep my house clean, I was no good at cooking etc. George and Gertie did not visit very often. They had three sons to bring up, and in any case George never did get on well with his family.

I missed my friends at the telegraph office. Sometimes one of the men would bring his wife along to tea, but they always had to go next door. Ken and Marcia. were a lovely couple. Ken worked in the same office as I had so he brought news of friends I had made there. After a year Ralph decided we were missing my money coming in, so Win decided to take a part time job. She worked in the morning so my afternoons were free. Her mother began to get ill so she gave up work altogether, I took a part-time job as a telephonist at the Moorfields Eye Hospital in High Holborn. I worked from 12 to 6. I really enjoyed the work, I felt I was being of some use to someone. One day who should walk into the hospital but Ken. I was pleased to see him. He did not know I was working there as I had not contacted him and Marcia for a while. He had something in his eye so he came to Casualty. He too had left the post office and was working in a firm near by.

One day when I was working at Moorfields, Mr. Hudson, one of the surgeons, asked me to ring a Paris number. I had to ask the person who answered to inform the Duke of Windsor that a room would be ready for him at King Edward the Seventh Hospital and would they please let the hospital know his expected time of arrival I got thorough very quickly and you can imagine my surprise when the Duke himself answered the phone. I can't remember whether I curtsied but it would have been difficult sitting down at the switchboard!

My mother-in-law was terrified of thunderstorms. As soon as she heard any thunder she would hide any knives that were about and cover her face with her apron. One day Ralph was painting the outside of her house when it came on to rain. He stood by the open door watching it, I joined him. Suddenly he made a disgusting noise. His mother called out to us to come in as it was thundering. We assured her it wasn't but she insisted we come in and shut the door. Ralph and I were in fits of laughter, his mother was sitting with her apron over her face and could not understand why we were laughing. We never enlightened her.

For sometime Beryl would hide under the table when a storm arose, my mother-in-law had passed that fear on to her. One day George happened to call when there was a storm. Seeing Beryl under the table he lifted her out and explained to her about storms. He told her that very few people were hurt or killed by storms. In time she lost her fear. It's funny how certain things stand out in one's memory more than others.

Mother's 80th birthday at Bognor in 1962
Back row from left Frank, Tony, Uncle Reg, Maureen Belcher, Gina, Derek
Middle from left Beryl, Phyllis, Muriel, Nn, Ruby, Dorrie, Dick, May, Bill
Holding Derek and Gina's daughter Carol
Front row from left Susan, Aunt Edie, Mother, Auntie May

In 1962 Mother celebrated her 80th birthday. Bruce took Beryl and me down to Bognor as May was giving a party for her. Bruce could not stop for the actual party as he was going to meet his young lady in Guildford, and they were going to do some conservation work. Dick and Susan were already down there but the rest of the family had hired a small coach to bring them. When it drew up and Mother saw everyone piling out she said to me "I know I am going to cry." I told her tears of happiness were the best ones to shed. Ralph did not come down, I don't know why. It was on a Sunday, I suppose he did not want to leave his mother although she wasn't on her own. Anyway we had a lovely day, the weather was perfect. Mother's two sisters were there, Auntie May, with her husband Reg, and Aunt Edie.

In 1963 tragedy struck again in our family. Frank's wife Nan died of stomach cancer. It was a very sad time for Frank. We all loved Nan, she was so full of fun.

In February the following year I went down to Bognor for the weekend on my own. May wrote and said mother was not too well, so I was determined to see her. Poor darling, she did look ill. She said she thought she had an ulcer in her stomach, at least that's what she told me.

I did not see her again until Bruce and Ellie got married in the May. It was a lovely wedding in a very attractive setting in Peaslake, near Guildford. When Mother arrived with May we were shocked at her condition. She was supposed to be in hospital but she told the doctor she wanted to come to her grandson's wedding. Bruce and Ellie were going to live in Scotland, he was going to be Warden of a Field Centre at Kindrogan near Pitlochry. A week after their wedding a policeman called to say Mother was very ill and was not expected to survive the night. Ralph saw me on the train at Victoria station to Chichester. It was a dreadful night, wind, rain, thunder, the lot. The journey was awful. Parts of the track were flooded so we were just crawling along at times. I felt we would never get there. I had no idea where the hospital was but there was a taxi waiting outside. I am afraid I almost pushed a man into the gutter as I was so desperate to get to the hospital. I explained to him about my mother and he was very kind. He said he hoped I would find things better than I thought they might be and then he helped me into the cab. I realised as soon as I got to the ward that Mother was dying. There were no other members of my family there and it wasn't until later I found out why. The sister took me to Mother then she brought me a very welcome cup of tea. Apparently Mother had had a stroke in the afternoon. When asked if any other members of my family had been in she said she did not know as she was night staff. I arrived at the hospital at midnight and Mother passed away peacefully an hour later. The doctor then told me Mother had cancer of the stomach. They were hoping to operate the next day but the stroke had taken her. He told me even if they had operated she would have been in a lot of pain and a permanent invalid. I told him that was the last thing Mother deserved so in the end Nature took its course. I remember giving her seven kisses, one from each of her children before the nurse led me away. I spent the night in a room in the hospital.

It was strange that I who had seen the least of her should be the one with her at the end. In my heart I was glad about that, although I spent the night crying my eyes out, worrying about how the others would take it. Just before I left the hospital in the morning Bill rang. The girl on duty gave me the phone so I was able to tell him about Mother. He was very surprised to hear my voice. I told him I was going straight to May, he said he would be there as soon as possible. He was spending a week in Devon, he did not want to go but Mother had insisted he had his holiday. She was one of the most unselfish people I have ever known and certainly one of the kindest. The journey from the hospital to May's cottage that morning was a nightmare. A terrific storm was overhead. I was worried sick as I knew May was frightened of storms. I need not have worried because when I got there she opened the door to me. Her face was a picture when she saw who it was. She guessed what I was going to tell her. As luck would have it Dick was with her. They both went to the hospital after Mother had the stroke, but the sister told them to go home and rest as there was nothing they could do as mother was unconscious.

I was very unhappy for a long time after mother died, it may have been guilt at not seeing her more often but I was a long time getting over her going.

9

1964-1976

A year after Bruce and Ellie's wedding Tony, (Muriel and John's son) married Barbara. It seemed the only way I was going to see my family was at weddings and funerals. After Mother's death I was determined to see more of them, rows or no rows.

The year of 1966 was another eventful one. Beryl did well with her A-levels and got a place at Nottingham University. My mother-in-law did not want her to go, she said she would miss her. I asked her if she didn't think that her dad and I would miss her too. I told Beryl she was going, she had worked hard to get this far. After all, Bruce had worked hard to get into Cambridge so why shouldn't Beryl go to Nottingham. My mother-in-law replied that she didn't think it was necessary for girls to go to college. She was such a stupid woman!

Fate plays funny tricks on us because my mother-in-law was taken ill and, for some time, refused to go into hospital. In the end the doctor took it upon himself to order an ambulance and sent her there. We were all worn out. I stayed home from work and spent most of the time washing her sheets. She died a week after being admitted. I am afraid I breathed a sigh of relief. I am no hypocrite and shed no tears. I did try hard to like Ralph's mother but she tried hard to wreck our marriage. Ralph took his mother's death very hard.

A week before Beryl went to Nottingham Dick and Ted celebrated their silver wedding. Ralph came with us. I was so glad he did. Beryl left at the end of September. We certainly missed her.

Ralph had a breakdown after his mother's death. He was ill for quite some time. In June 1967 we went on our first holiday on our own since our marriage. We had a wonderful fortnight in Bournemouth. This really helped Ralph to recover. Ralph had left the buses some time before his mother's death and was manager of a small department store in Clapton.

Soon after Tony's wedding May left Bognor and came to live in London very near Bill and Dorrie, and Muriel and John. In fact Muriel's 'lollipop' position was almost opposite May's flat. May managed to get a clerical job near by. I was able to see much more of my family and, when possible, Ralph came with me. He only had Thursday afternoons and Sundays off, the same as when we had been courting years earlier.

Beryl was 21 in September 1968, we gave her a lovely party which was also celebrated her engagement to Malcolm. They had met in University. He was studying computer science and Beryl was studying sociology. Malcolm was a year older than her and so was one year ahead of her.

On April 17 1967 Ellie presented Bruce with a dear little daughter, Hazel Jean. How thrilled Ralph and I were to become grandparents. That same year when Hazel was few months old they left Scotland and lived in Kings Langley, in Hertfordshire for four years. Bruce was Conservation Officer in Hertfordshire and also taught at Rickmansworth Grammar School. The following year Frank introduced his new lady friend to the family. We all gathered at May's flat. What a shock Joan must have had seeing us all gathered there waiting to be introduced. Joan was headmistress of an infants' school. She and Frank had met at their church. She was an entirely different person to Nan. Joan was much quieter and, to us, not so much fun.

Ralph had been unwell for sometime with breathing problems. We went to the London Chest hospital to see a specialist. He told Ralph he must give up smoking. He showed us the x-ray they had taken of his lungs. There was a nasty great blob on one of them.

That summer Ralph and I went to spend a holiday with Muriel and John who had left London and bought a bungalow at Loddiswell in south Devon. Neither one of us had been to Devon before. John met us at the station and I just sat enthralled as we went along. I had never seen such lovely scenery. The quietness and beauty of the area was marvellous. John took us to some beautiful parts of Devon. When we got back our children told us to go and live there!

In 1969 Beryl got her degree, a second class honours in Social Sciences. She had decided to live in Manchester where she had been offered a job. In the October she married Malcolm. Before she left on their honeymoon she begged me to persuade Ralph to give up work, sell the house and move down to Devon. Bruce also told Ralph that he should think about it. When we said it would mean we were a long way away from them they said there was such a thing as transport. They could come to us and we could visit them.

In the April of 1970 we went back to Devon and found the very place we wanted. It was in Kingsbridge just three miles from Loddiswell. We were told we could move in at the end of August, so I gave my notice in at the beginning of the month and left the following week. In the second week of August we got a letter from the estate agents to say we could not move in until September 12th as the buyers could not get a mortgage until then. This upset us both very badly as you can imagine. We were almost packed up by then. This had a very bad effect on Ralph because he had a heart attack. We were dreadfully worried in case he could not get down to Devon. We did eventually make it but only with instructions from our doctor to enrol with a doctor in Devon as soon as possible.

Not long before we moved down to Devon Bruce took Ralph and me to Scotland. He was going to run a fungus foray and wanted us to see how beautiful Scotland was. We spent a few nights in hotels on the way, eventually arriving at Kindrogan, the place where he and Ellie came when they were first married. There were about sixty people in the party from all over the world and all walks of life. It was a wonderful experience. I shall never forget the grandeur of the scenery. I remember going to Moulin Moor quite early one morning, the sun was glistening on the silver webs covering the heather. It was a sight so beautiful, one I shall never forget. I have been back to Scotland with Beryl and Malcolm and Bruce and Ellie since, but have never managed to catch the wonder of that first visit with Bruce.

When we arrived at our new home Muriel and John were waiting on the verandah to greet us with the key to the door. May was coming down to help us move in. She was a great help. When May left Bill came down for a fortnight and helped Ralph rebuild the kitchen. What fun we had one way or another. This was the beginning of a very happy period of our life. I felt I had at last found my haven and Ralph, I know, felt the same. We pleased ourselves what we did without interference from our in-laws.

In 1972 May retired from work, she wanted to come to Devon too. Ralph and I managed to find her a very nice ground floor flat about fifteen minutes walk away from us. The owner wanted someone who would look after her garden for her. She was an elderly lady and lived in the flat upstairs. We told her my sister was a professional gardener and in January, May moved in.

This year Bruce and Ellie moved up to North Wales. Bruce got a job as a lecturer in Chester College. They bought a house in Mold. Hazel stayed with us while they were moving. We both adored her. In March of this same year Ron and Pam moved down to Kingsbridge. We found them a house two doors away from us. We always got on well with Ron and Pam and we loved the children. Those first two years we had a lot of visitors. We did not mind because some of them helped Ralph with the decorating. One of his cousins dug the vegetable garden for him. I had to watch that Ralph did not overdo things. Ralph and I were the happiest we had been all our married life. We would take the bus into Plymouth or go for walks along the estuary. Sometimes May would come with us.

Soon after May moved down Muriel was taken ill. She had a very serious operation for cancer in March and in October she had a hysterectomy. She was backwards and forwards to Plymouth for sometime after that but, thank God, she fully recovered.

I joined the Old Time Dancing Club with Muriel. It was held in our local hotel every Monday evening. Ralph did not like dancing so he stayed at home. When Adrian moved down with his parents he would come and keep his uncle company. After a while May joined us. She would spend the night at our house as we did not like her walking home on her own. John would come and pick Muriel up. Every July there is a carnival in Kingsbridge. It is great fun. When Ralph and I first saw it, with the people dancing in the street and all the beautiful floats we thought we were in another world. We had never seen any thing like it.

George and Gertie came one day, they were having a holiday in Cornwall. Before they left they told me Ralph said he wished he had left Clapton years ago. He had realised what a life I had had. He told them he could never make up for the past 30 years. Well, now we were very happy together and I never once criticised his mother to him.

In June 1973 Bruce and Ellie had a fine son, Gareth Douglas. How delighted we were to have a grandson. They brought him down to us in the October. It was wonderful having our grandchildren around us. Hazel adored her baby brother.

Just before Christmas Ralph had another slight heart attack.

At Christmas that year Beryl and Malcolm came to visit us, also Bill, Dorrie, Dorrie's sister, Ida and a long standing friend of the family, Ruby. We all went round to May for Christmas dinner, the first Christmas we had spent with my own family since we were married. We did enjoy ourselves. Our Auntie May and Uncle Reg were living in Stokenham, a village near us, so they joined us for tea on Boxing Day. Uncle Reg had taken Ralph and I out for some lovely rides. He took us on our first visit to Cornwall.

During Beryl and Malcolm's visit over the Christmas she told us she was pregnant. How thrilled we were especially since a specialist had told Malcolm he wouldn't be able to father a child. They had been married for four years. After they went home Ralph and I talked a lot about our girlie (as he called her) becoming a mother

We had made friends with our next-door neighbours, Doris and Edwin Pinhay, they were a very nice couple indeed. On the evening of January 6th 1974 they invited us in for a drink and a game of cards. We thoroughly enjoyed ourselves. We both went to bed very happy that night. At ten o'clock the next morning my darling Ralph was dead. He had had a massive heart attack. I could not believe it when the doctor told me he had gone. May and Muriel were a great comfort to me that week. Muriel stayed with me all the time. Ron, Pam and the children were also very supportive. It was a great shock to us all. I am only pleased Ralph did not suffer. I said I did not want Beryl to come to the funeral as she was at a crucial time of her pregnancy. After the funeral I went back with Bruce. When we got to his house Ellie told me Hazel wanted to sleep with me as she did not think I ought to be on my own. I did not mind. I was greatly touched and welcomed the idea of having her company. When I went to bed Hazel said that If I wanted anything in the night, a drink or something, I wasn't to worry, she would get it for me. I don't know how I kept back the tears. Before we went to sleep Hazel asked me where Grandpa was. Ellie said she would probably ask a lot of questions, especially as one of her friend's grandfather had died the week before and had been buried. She told Mummy she hoped Grandpa wasn't going to be put under the ground. I told her to get out of bed and look out of the window and see if there were any stars shining. We saw one or two. Then I told her that soon Grandpa would be up there shining on us and watching us. I remember she gave me a lovely kiss and said she would take care of me while I was staying with her. What a comfort she was to me. She was only six years old. I will never forget that night. Talk about a little child shall lead them. Hazel softened the blow of Ralph's death for me. When I came home Adrian and Julia, (Ron and Pam's children) had decided between them to come and stay alternate nights with me. Adrian took his uncle's death very badly.

I took up the threads of my life again and continued to go to Old Time Dancing.

In August, Susan (Dick's daughter) married Peter. This same year Uncle Reg died and Auntie May passed away in 1975. Bert's son Christopher also died that year, while on a fact-finding tour of the United states. He had been a District Attorney in Sydney. We were told he had had a heart attack; he was only thirty years old and left a young family.

In the June of this year Bill rang me. (I had the phone put in soon after Ralph died.) He asked me if I would like to go to Jersey with Dorrie in the August. He said he would pay for my flight if I could manage to pay for my hotel for the week. I jumped at the idea although I had never flown before and was really quite scared at the idea. We had a lovely holiday, the weather was perfect. I did not mind the flight back, but going I asked Dorrie if we had left the ground. She laughed at me and said yes, some fifteen minutes ago!

Soon after this I was approached by someone and asked if I would like to be a committee member for the Conservative Party constituency. Never having been on a committee before I was a bit dubious about joining. I'm glad I did join because I made many friends and really enjoyed the meetings. It gave me a new outlook on life. Muriel was already a member of her Loddiswell branch.

On the 27th of June 1974 Beryl had a son Euan. How thrilled I was for her. The following year on August 31st she had a second son, Neil.

In 1976 Bill went to visit Bert in Australia. We were all eager to hear about his visit on his return. This was the first time any member of the family had seen him since he went to Sydney in 1947. Although members of the family had spoken to him at Christmas for years no one had been able to see him.

That same year May married Bill Highfield. He ran the Old Time Dancing Club. This was May's first time round so to speak. How happy we all were for her. They had a very nice wedding and May moved into Bill's lovely bungalow in Stokenham. May had had many boyfriends in her life. She was a very attractive girl and full of fun. She was 65 when she married. Mother would have been delighted if she had been alive. Bill had been married before, twice in fact. He had a son and a stepson. They were fond of May, and, for the first time in her life, she could have anything she wanted, as Bill was quite well off.

Also in this year Malcolm (Beryl's husband) had a very bad accident. He was thrown off his motorbike and received very serious injuries to his leg and chest. I went up to Manchester to help look after the two children. He was in hospital for several months. I stayed up there until he was moved from intensive care to a general ward. As luck would have it they were able to save his leg.

The following year Dick and Ted became grandparents. Susan and Peter had a son, Gavin. Three years later Emma was born. What a lot of grandchildren and great-grandchildren Mother and Dada would have had!

10

1977-1989

For the next two years I saw a lot of Bill and May. They took me out in their car quite often, so did Muriel and John. My children would bring their families down on holiday and I would visit them.

In February 1979 Bill rang me and said Dorrie had been taken to hospital following a heart attack. I packed my bag and went to stay in London. I stayed with Bill for two weeks until Dorrie came home, then their friend, Ruby, came and took over. Although Dorrie's sister was living with them she was a lot older than Dorrie and her sight was very bad, so she could not help Bill very much. I left Dorrie looking and feeling much better. She did not want me to leave but I promised I would be back in a week or two. Before I left Ruby asked me if there were any houses for sale in Kingsbridge as she very much wanted to move down there from Watford. I told her I would certainly see what I could do. In any case she arranged to spend Easter with me. A week before Easter I had another phone call from Bill. He told me Dorrie had passed away quite suddenly while talking on the phone. It was a shock because we all thought she was getting better. Again I went to London to be with Bill. Ruby came as well, to help. Before we went back to Devon, Bill asked us if we would look out for a house to take him, Ida and Ruby, as they had talked things over and decided they would all like to come down. Bill had always loved Devon.

We were lucky. The very next day after arriving home May rang me and said there was a house advertised in our local paper quite near me, and would I go and case the joint! It was a lovely house standing in its own grounds with a conservatory and a greenhouse. I rang May back and said how lovely it was, from the outside at least. The outcome was that Bill, and Ruby came down to view it the next day, fell in love with it, and decided to have it. I was thrilled to bits, more of my family was coming to live near me. They managed to sell their houses quite quickly. I went up to London and Watford to help them pack. I was as excited as they were. It is not that Bill didn't feel the loss of Dorrie, of course he did, they had been married for 49 years, after all. He said he would have moved down to Devon a long time ago but Dorrie did not like the quietness of the country.

One very important thing happened in 1979. Bruce got his PhD. I went up for this great occasion which was held in the Philharmonic Hall in Liverpool. Unless you have experienced the thrill of seeing your son or daughter receiving the degree they have worked so hard to get, you cannot imagine the pride you can feel in your children. My only regret was that his father was not there to see him. We did both see him graduate from Cambridge and Beryl from Nottingham. Soon after Ellie went to college to get her BA. She was a student at Chester College where Bruce lectured.

In July Beryl and Malcolm had their third son, David. How pleased I was for them. Their family was now complete. I now had 4 lovely grandsons and a charming granddaughter.

Bill, Ida and Ruby moved down to Devon in July. There were many helping hands to assist their moving in. In October Bill and Ruby married. This was Ruby's first marriage. She was 74. All the family were delighted to know Bill was going to be well looked after and loved again. During their wedding reception a phone call came from Bert in Australia. Someone had arranged with the hotel to accept the call. Bill said it made their day.

It was great living so near to Bill and Ruby, just five minutes walk away. The first Christmas Ruby said she would like us all to go to them for Christmas Day. There were twelve of us altogether. It was the first time she had put on a Christmas dinner for so many people, she did us proud. She had never made a Christmas pudding and was a bit dubious about it, so, in the end that was my job. Muriel made one of her famous sponges and May contributed something as well. A good time was has by all.

In 1982 Frank became very ill with Guillain-Barré Syndrome. He was in hospital for many months. The following January Bill and Ruby visited Bert and his family in Australia. I don't think they had met Ruby before, but apparently got on very well together. But then one could not help liking Bert. I took care of Ida while they were away. Before they came back to Devon they visited Frank in hospital.

He was getting better by then but was still very weak.

In 1983 Muriel and I went to Bournemouth. One evening whilst I was having a bath before getting ready to dress for dinner I got stuck. I called Muriel to help but the rotter just stood there laughing. She said she would get a porter to come and assist me. In the end we managed between us with a lot of laughter as you can imagine. We were very late down to the dining room and when our table mates asked if anything was wrong my terrible sister told the whole company about my predicament. You can guess the teasing I got.

My friends Ken and Marcia come into the picture again. After we came back from Bournemouth they came down for a holiday. They did not have a car but we went for some nice bus rides. We had meals with different members of the family. They were a very popular couple, surrounded by laughter. We really were a very happy family as I have said before. I can never remember any of us falling out with one another.

In 1984 Bill's sister-in-law Ida died, so now Bill and Ruby felt they could go where they liked so they came on holiday with Muriel and me. It was one week of hilarity. We had never been on holiday with Bill since Dada died.

In June 1985 Frank and Joan moved down to Kingsbridge. Joan was not to happy about it at first, but later on she was glad, because her brother moved down to Chillington, about three miles away. Frank and Joan had a modern bungalow about twenty minutes walk away from Bill and me. Frank joined the local camera club, also the Conservative Committee, of which he became the treasurer. So there were now five of us Eaton children living within a three-mile radius, wonderful! Soon after Frank moved down May and Bill moved from Stokenham and came to Kingsbridge. They lived a few minutes walk from Frank. We knew Dick did not want to leave Windsor. She came down at least twice a year and stayed with one or the other of us.

Not long after Bill and Ruby moved down, Mr Spry, a gentleman living a few doors away from me started to organise coach trips for the people in our area. We went to see some lovely houses and lots of gardens. One trip was to Slimbridge Wildfowl Trust, which was very interesting. Another time we went to Buckland Abbey. Here there were a lot of Sir Francis Drake's treasures. We went to the beautiful gardens ot Stourhead and Killerton, near Exeter. Bill and Ruby did enjoy these outings, especially the gardens. Most of these were National Trust properties and were well looked after. We went on trips to many parts of Cornwall. Dick came with us once or twice, also Ken and Marcia, when they happened to be down on holiday with me. Sometimes we would have a trip over Dartmoor. Twice we went to Robin Hanbury Tennyson's lovely house on Bodmin Moor. He is an explorer and he showed us many of the treasures he had brought back with him from his travels. He really is a very interesting person to meet. Sometimes I was able to go on Muriel's outings with the Loddiswell over sixties club. I must say I had never been to so many places in my life before I moved to Devon. I did not go out much when I was living in London. I only wish Ralph had lived long enough so he could join me on these outings. We also went to Seaton one day on one of Muriel's trips and we took the little tram from Seaton to Colyton, a lovely little village. That was really something to remember. Unfortunately Mr Spry died quite suddenly and no one came forward to take his place. He really was a good organiser. He would go to the place before us and find out where the toilets were, (very important for us oldies!) He would also find out where the best eating places were and would book us in, if it was for tea only. He was a good and thoughtful man. and was certainly missed by us all.

I must tell you about an incident that happened one dance night. It was a dinner dance, full evening dress etc. Muriel and I were dancing together, laughing together as usual, when my bottom teeth fell out on the dance floor and slid under a row of chairs. The more I tried to pick them up the more they slid away. The place was in an uproar. They had to stop the dance while I retrieved them and dashed out to the cloakroom to wash them. Every one saw the funny side of it and I was laughing to much to feel embarrassed.

One day in 1985 Muriel rang me and said in future I was to treat her with respect. On asking why she informed me she had been made President of the over sixties club. I was delighted for her. Every month she writes a report in our local paper about what the club has done that month. One year she opened the Loddiswell fete. I went along to support her. She made a nice opening speech and I felt proud of her.

The following year Ted died. We were very upset, he was such a nice man. Dick did not want us to go to his funeral. She said it was too far for us to travel in one day. He was greatly missed in the family. When he came down on holiday he would walk for miles with us. He was a lot older than Dick and must have been nearly ninety when he died. Dick hated living on her own, so Susan and Peter gave up their home and went to live with her. I am sure Gavin and Emma were a great comfort to her. In 1987 Joan became very ill and died of liver cancer. This really was a blow, coming so soon after Ted's death. I stayed with Frank for a week after the funeral to try and help him come to terms with his loss. He became more involved with his camera club and won quite a few prizes in competitions. Frank and Bill both kept lovely gardens and the two men would spend a lot of time together, helping one another.

In 1988 Muriel and John celebrated their Golden Wedding anniversary, the only members of the family to do so. Of course there was the usual party.

11

1990-1993

Now we come to 1990. Ken wrote saying Marcia was far from well. Frank was also seeing the doctor pretty regularly. He did not say what was wrong, neither did Ken. In October I got shingles.

Phyllis and Muriel on their 80th birthday in 1990

On November 24th Muriel and I celebrated our 80th birthday. We had a wonderful party in our local church hall. Our children decorated the hall and then sent us both home while they sorted the tables out. In the mean time the press arrived. Our photos were in the local paper. I knew that, in time, we would become famous! There were nearly fifty guests. John's brother Roy was the Master of Ceremonies and Frank organised the music for dancing etc. Bruce recorded the song, "Its my mother's birthday today." I could see that neither Frank nor Marcia were very well. Marcia's son made a video of that evening. It really was a smashing time.

That Christmas Muriel and John went up to Tony and Barbara's home near Halifax. The rest of us decided we would have Christmas dinner in a hotel. We went to a lovely little place in Marlborough, near Salcombe. Frank did not join us as he was not well enough. We went back afterwards to his place for a cup of tea and some cake. In the New Year Frank really became ill. He, like Joan, had liver cancer. I spent as much time as I could with him, and I slept at his house for the last week he was at home; it was dreadful seeing him in so much pain. A week before Easter he was admitted to Derriford Hospital in Plymouth. Two days later I was admitted to the Eye infirmary in Plymouth for a cataract operation. On Easter Sunday Frank's nephew and niece brought him to see me in hospital. We sat holding hands and he told me he was dying and he had left a letter for us all, Bert as well. I just don't know how I controlled myself, my heart was breaking at the sight of him. He did not stay long, but when he kissed me he said I wouldn't see him any more. After he had gone I just flung myself on the bed and let the tears come. The nurses were so kind. I was frightened I would undo the good that had been done to my eye. They assured me crying would not hurt. How sweet they all were in he ward. The day I came out of hospital Beryl came down to take me home. Before doing so she took me to see Frank once again. He was getting ready to go to St. Luke's Hospice in Plymouth. Beryl helped him pack his things up. That was the last I saw of my lovely brother. We had to delay his funeral for a month as Frank expressly wished that his friend, a vicar from his London church, should conduct the funeral service.

I call 1991 our year of sorrow. In January Dick went to visit Bert in Australia. When she came back she said he was very ill. Two weeks after Frank's funeral John was found dead, he had hanged himself in the garage. What a dreadful shock that was. I was so distraught for my Muriel I could not go to her. I knew that she had a friend staying with her. I went round to Bill who had told me what had happened. We were crying on each others shoulders, Ruby as well. I could not believe it. He had seemed alright at Frank's funeral but he had been suffering from severe back pain and could not face being old. When Tony and Barbara came down from Halifax they came to see me. I said I could not go to see Muriel as I would not have been much comfort to her. Tony came and fetched me the day after anyway. Muriel and I were very strong, we did not cry once when we were together. The local church was packed for John's funeral, this was some comfort for Muriel. I should think half the village of Loddiswell turned out. John had been on the Parish Council and he belonged to the local Ramblers' Association.

That was not the end of our troubles for in July May's husband, Bill, died of a stroke and Bert died of cancer around the same time. His funeral was being conducted on the same day as Bill's. May was becoming more and more vague so after Bill's death she came to stay with me. This was a very trying time indeed, the poor darling had Alzheimer's disease. I looked after her for eight weeks before we could get her into a home. My sympathies go out to anyone who has to look after this kind of patient. At times May was really nasty to me. I just kept telling myself that it wasn't May talking, that she would never hurt any of us. In the beginning of October May was admitted to a lovely home, Westlands, on the outskirts of Kingsbridge. The staff were wonderful to her. At times she would know us when we visited her, which was quite often, then we would laugh together. The funny thing was that May was apparently always laughing, most of the other people would look sad and miserable. I think that is why the staff grew so fond of her.

The beginning of 1992 was not much better than the previous year because Ron died of emphysema. He had been in hospital in Plymouth but they sent him to our local one just a few minutes walk away from where we were living. The end was sudden. Once again the church was full. For many years Ron had been a town, district and county councillor and was much respected for the work he did on behalf of the local communities and for charities.

In February Marcia died; she had been ill with cancer of the mouth. Poor Ken was devastated. There seemed no end to our mourning. On reading these last pages they seem rather morbid, but I am writing about the lives of my family and friends. The larger the family one has the more loved ones there are to mourn over. In July I went to spend a fortnight with Ken in Chichester. I thought I might be able to help him out of his depression. He told me afterwards I had. Unfortunately I became ill while I was staying with him. I could not seem to breathe properly. Ken was extremely worried. He did not know whether to get his own doctor to see me or wait for me to go home and see my own. We decided on the latter option. I travelled home by coach and when I arrived at Plymouth I almost collapsed. I did not wait for the bus but got a taxi all the way to Kingsbridge. The driver kept asking me if I was OK. He was very kind. As soon as I got home on Wednesday I called my doctor. He could not fathom what was wrong with me. Bill rang Muriel and her neighbour brought her over right away. She then rang Beryl who came down the next day. She and Malcolm were supposed to be going to Scotland on the Friday. She cancelled that immediately she knew I was ill. Bruce and Ellie were in Switzerland with Hazel, who was studying at the Berne Conservatoire. I was taken to Plymouth on

Sunday morning and was diagnosed as having blood clots on both lungs. No wonder I had felt so ill.

I was in Derriford Hospital, Plymouth for eleven days then transferred to our local cottage hospital where I stayed for another eleven days. Beryl brought Muriel in to see me and sometimes Bill and Ruby. Bruce and Ellie had kept in touch with the hospital staff who advised them not to curtail their holiday. They drove straight to Muriel from the ferry the day they got back to England and came to fetch me from the local hospital and take me to Muriel's house to recuperate. When I saw them enter the ward I could not believe my eyes, it was a real tonic. I stayed with Muriel for another two weeks. She really helped me to get on my feet again, and thoroughly spoiled me.

The Social Services people in Kingsbridge were very good. They had an extra stair rail put in and arranged for a lifeline telephone to be installed. This was actually done by the British Legion, which was cheaper for me. What a boon it was. I came home for good on the 2nd of September. My doctor kept his eye on me for a while and called in frequently.

In October Gareth started as a student at Brunel University, just outside London. He was studying Music and Geology, as he wanted to be a rock musician! Unfortunately he contracted glandular fever the following year. He was poorly for some time and when he returned to the college he found the curriculum had changed and, as it was not what he wanted, he left.

In 1993 Hazel returned home from Switzerland with a very good degree. She had made many friends out there, as did her parents. She is an oboist.

By now I had someone in to do the cleaning for me. I was advised not to do any heavy work for a time after coming out of hospital. I had never been used to having someone work for me before but it certainly made life much easier to have a very nice lady, Judy, to do the cleaning.

Ken came down on holiday in August and we had a lovely time together. He said he would like to marry me, but I did not want to leave Kingsbridge where my family was, especially Muriel, and he did not want to leave Chichester, where his son lived. Ken also said he could not bear it if I became ill like Marcia. We remained good friends and were always on the phone to one another, until he became too ill. We visited May about once a week but we could see the deterioration in her. Sometimes she would have no idea who we were. Dick came down in autumn and visited May two or three times. It seemed so sad to see our laughing happy sister sitting there not knowing what day it was or who we were.

In November Bill had to return to Derriford Hospital again for x-rays, his prostate was clearly not behaving itself. That Christmas Bill, Ruby and I went to Muriel. She is such a wonderful hostess, nothing is too much trouble for her. We always enjoyed her culinary efforts. We missed talking to Bert and Christmas wasn't the same without the rest of the family.

When the rest of the family moved down we celebrated our birthdays with a get-together at the birthday person's house. After Frank and the other members died these dates became very flat. On Bill and Ruby's wedding anniversary we generally ended up at the Cottage Hotel in Hope Cove for a meal. This is a lovely hotel, I would say the best in the South Hams. For our birthdays we still met up too, but there was certainly a gap.

When I reached my 80th birthday I gave up my committee work. I did not like coming home in the dark. I still keep in touch with some of the friends I made. Muriel left her committee a couple of years later.

In November the town put on an Extravaganza, in other words an evening carnival where the floats are all lit up. It was a wonderful sight. Some of the floats came from as far afield as Somerset. This was the first time we had had such a show and it was a huge success. They have one every year now.

1993 was an exciting year for Muriel and I. We have both been very keen on writing poetry but never had any published, until one day Muriel rang me and told me a firm in Peterborough were looking for poems from people in the West country. The long and the short of it is that since then we have dozens of poems published between us. We do not get paid for them but the royalties from books sold go to charity. It was great fun seeing our names in print. I think our families were rather proud of us. In recent years some of our poems have been reprinted in small books, for instance, to celebrate our 90th birthday.

Dick came down in the Spring and we were able to go on one of Muriel's outings. We went to Looe and had a lovely day. When I came home I found one of the bedrooms had flooded. Apparently one of the old pipes in the loft had burst. I was glad Dick was with me. We mopped up what we could and at 11.30 that night I rang my plumber. He came round straight away and turned the water off. The place was a mess. The next morning the plumber was back again at 8am. He took the carpet up and fitted a new plastic pipe, not lead like the old one. We were very lucky in Kingsbridge, the workmen didn't overcharge. Anyway Dick and I had a good laugh about it because it had been raining all the way home from Looe so, as Dick said, "A little more water didn't hurt!"

In October Muriel and I went to Falmouth for a week. We stayed at a big hotel near the front. We were very lucky because a coach party were down the same week and as there were seats to spare they took Muriel and I on a couple of their trips. One was to the seal centre in Gweek. That was fascinating. One evening the proprietors hired a conjurer to entertain us. He was very clever. He called me out to help him with one of his tricks. I still can't fathom out where the rabbit came from, even though I was standing right next to him!

In the November Bill was back again in Derriford Hospital for more x-rays.

12

1994-1996

Adrian, Ron's adopted son, used to come and do my garden for me. Mind you, he did not know a rose from a dandelion, but at least he kept it tidy for me by cutting back the shrubs. Adrian had been in the Navy for 12 years and went all over the world. During this time he was married, and divorced. I have always been fond of him and he would confide in me, knowing it would go no further. I think I was the only one who shed tears when I saw him off to Plymouth, when he first joined the Navy. Julia is married to a sailor and has two children. Her husband, Michael, is a Chief Petty Officer but never served on the same ship as Adrian.

October was a very happy month. In the early part of the month Dick came to spend a week in Falmouth with us. What fun we had. The weather could have been better, but it didn't keep us in. There was an indoor swimming pool at the hotel and Dick went in most days. I would have joined her but unfortunately I caught a heavy cold the day after we arrived and Muriel was not very keen on swimming. Before dinner on our first evening Dick said she wanted to take a picture of her room from the beach. Down we trooped to the seafront. Dick was all poised with her camera when we pointed out she was focussing on the wrong window. Amid a lot of laughter she finally managed to take the photograph she wanted. Alas they never came out.

We were enjoying out first holiday with Dick since leaving school. It was one round of laughter.

Bruce came for me and took me home to Mold. On the Saturday we all went to Manchester to celebrate Beryl and Malcolm's Silver Wedding. It was a lovely surprise party which their church organised for them. When they came to the hall it was all in darkness but when someone put the lights on there were about seventy people waiting to greet them. The expression on Beryl's face was a picture, especially when she saw me sitting there with Hazel and Ellie. Bruce came on later. He was giving a lecture in Huddersfield that evening and could not change the date. After the party Beryl and Malcolm went to Paris for the weekend. I spent a very nice time with Bruce and Ellie.

At the beginning of November Bill went to Bristol Infirmary for a special x-ray and I stayed with Ruby until Bill came home a few days later. All seemed well, thank goodness. We spent Christmas with Muriel, Tony and Barbara. This was another year with its ups and downs.

One day Adrian came to me in a rather perturbed state. He had received a letter from Dr. Barnado's about his adoption. Apparently his birth mother wanted to get in touch with him. I asked him if that was what he wanted and he said he wasn't sure, although he had recently thought about his real mother a lot. Pam, naturally, was not too pleased about this, but Adrian was over 30 and entitled to make up his own mind. Quite frankly I was pleased for him and told him so. He eventually met his real mother and they clicked at once. Again, Pam took this badly, so much so that she asked Maureen (his birth mother) to come down and meet her. I am afraid Pam could have made things easier for them. I know how she must have felt. She had brought Adrian up and now this stranger had come along wanting to know him. I took to Maureen and was thrilled for her. It seems she had been raped at the age of 16 and her mother made her have the baby adopted. Adrian went to live near her but the relationship ran into difficulties and they are no longer in touch. Adrian now lives in Sussex and has not, on reflection, had a happy life. I miss seeing him. Although Julia is adopted too she has no desire to find her real mother.

That Easter I went to stay with Beryl and Malcolm. Beryl came to fetch Muriel and I. Tony picked Muriel up from Beryl's house. Our families fix things among themselves as to who will fetch us and return us home and they won't let us travel on our own. They are all so thoughtful. I have been to some wonderful places when I have been staying with them. I've also been some very good shows. While I was at Beryl's that Easter Bill rang to say that Ruby has been taken to Derriford Hospital. Her legs had broken out in sores. This was the first time Ruby had ever been in hospital, she was four months short of her 90th birthday. Poor darling, she did not like it very much. She was very deaf and could not understand what was being said. Luckily, she was only in for 2 or 3 days.

After Easter, Hazel came and picked me up from Beryl's and took me to Mold. On the Friday we went to listen to listen to St. Matthew's Passion in a lovely little church in the village of Tremeirchion, among the Clwydian Hills, a few miles away. Hazel was playing in the orchestra. It was a beautiful performance.

At the beginning of May I had a phone call from Sue to say that Dick was in hospital. Adrian took Bill, Muriel and I up to see her in hospital. She was very ill. We were all very worried for her. Unfortunately our darling Dick suffered a stroke and passed away on the 23rd. It was a terrible blow. We just could not imagine life without Dick Adrian was very good. He took us up to the funeral. Ruby did not come. She said she would be alright on her own all day. How glad Muriel and I were that we had the holiday in Falmouth with her the year before. It was certainly something to remember her by.

In August Sue, Peter and Emma came down for a few days. This was the month we celebrated Ruby's 90th birthday. We all went to lunch at the Cottage Hotel. About this time I was beginning to have difficulty in swallowing. I could not understand it as I felt well in myself.

August was another exciting month. Beryl came to fetch me. I spent a couple of days with her then Bruce came to take me to Mold for a week. He took me to Anglesey one day to see the Sea Zoo which was very interesting. After a week Bruce took me back to Manchester because Beryl and Malcolm were taking me to the Norfolk Broads for another week's holiday. I had never been there before. We were also there to meet Euan's future in-laws. They live in a lovely little village called Mulbarton. Euan was engaged to Ruth whom he met when she went to visit her brother at Nottingham University, where Euan was a student. The next day we had a lovely boat trip on the Broads. What a gorgeous day it was. We visited Norwich Cathedral another day. I was still having trouble swallowing, and was beginning to get worried but I tried not to show it.

In October Bruce came down. He could see how distressed I was getting with my throat problem so he brought me a liquidiser so that my food would not have lumps in it. During his stay I was admitted to the eye infirmary for a cataract operation on the other eye. All went well. Soon after Mrs Low, the Manager, rang from Westlands Nursing Home to say May wasn't very well. The doctor had seen her and was coming again the next day. I asked if I should come and see her, but she did not think she was too bad. The following morning she rang again to tell me that May had died in the night. So we had lost two sisters in a few months.

Soon after May's funeral I went to see my doctor about my throat problem. He got me a quick appointment at Derriford Hospital for an x-ray. I was admitted a week before Christmas. I had my throat stretched and a biopsy taken. The next day I was told all was well, the biopsy proved nothing was wrong. I felt on top of the world over Christmas, my throat was fine, apart from a little soreness.

1996 started very badly for me. I was called back to Derriford hospital and was told by a specialist that I had cancer of the oesophagus. I was absolutely dumbfounded. Anyone who has been told that kind of news knows how I felt. I told the doctor I was informed in December that all was well, that I had nothing to worry about. He was very sympathetic and said they had looked at my tests again and found cancer cells. It must be just as bad for a doctor to have to tell a patient as a patient to hear it. I was not going to tell my family at first, then I thought how silly that would be as I knew they would all be very supportive. As soon as Muriel knew she got a friend to bring her to me. She stayed for a few of days. What a comfort she was. While she was there my doctor called one evening and explained things to me and also had a chat to Bruce on the phone. This was very comforting for me. In the beginning of February Bruce and Hazel came down and took me to see another specialist at Derriford. He told me they were going to give me pure alcohol injections into the tumour to shrink it. I had never heard of that before, neither had Bruce.

While Bruce and Hazel were with me I decided that I would have a new kitchen which I had been wanting for ages. They helped me choose all the cupboards and fittings and I ordered it. My next door neighbour was a builder and he agreed to fit the units when they arrived and refurbish the kitchen. It looked very good. Hazel went home a couple of days later and, on the Monday I was admitted to hospital for my first treatment. Bruce came with me and stayed until the evening. He had a word with the doctor who said all was well. Bruce took me home the next day then went home himself. I was so glad of his company. Muriel came again for a few days to help me. How lucky I am to have a sister like her. I was backwards and forwards every so often to Derriford for further injections. I would just stay one night. I tried not to let the cancer bother me. I called the tumour "Thora" because it was in my thorax – that did amuse the specialist!

One day I was sitting by my bed in the hospital when the physiotherapist came and asked me to sit on the bed as he wanted to test my lungs. After thumping my back and nearly knocking it through to my front, he said, "O.K., I'll be along this afternoon." I told him that he needn't bother! I was reading my book after lunch when a man came and sat on my bed. I glanced up and thought it was a different physiotherapist. I said, "I suppose you want me on the bed." He turned to me and introduced himself as the hospital Chaplain! "Oh dear," I said, "I thought you were the therapist." We both laughed together. I saw that he had a prayer book with him and thought that he about to say one for me, but just then the physiotherapist came along. "Oh good," said the Chaplain, "this lady thought I wanted her on the bed! I told her I had been called many things but never a therapist before!" After a lots of laughter the two men went straight to the nurses' station and told them about me. No wonder the Chaplain did not open the prayer book, he probably thought that I was beyond help! There is a sequel to this story. In the evening Beryl brought Muriel to see me and one their way in they met a vicar. "Are you going to Tavy Ward?" asked Muriel. "I expect so," he replied. "Well," said Muriel, "if you see Phyllis Ing there she is my twin sister, so don't think it was I who asked you if you wanted me on the bed." The man looked puzzled. Later Muriel told me about the conversation. "What was he like?" I asked. Muriel described him and I burst out laughing. This wasn't the Chaplain but a Roman Catholic priest. Although I was in and out of the hospital for several years after this incident I was never visited by a clergyman again!

At the end of February Euan and Ruth got married. We all went to Norfolk. Muriel and I went with Beryl and Malcolm and stayed for a week in a bungalow by the sea. Unfortunately the weather was bitterly cold with snow and ice everywhere. The day of the wedding turned out very wet. Ruth made a lovely bride and we all enjoyed ourselves. Beryl made and iced their beautiful three- tiered cake.

In July Muriel and I had a lovely holiday in the Isle of Wight, with perfect weather. In August my dear Ken came down for a week. At the end of the month Bill and Ruby went to Jersey. Bill had to push Ruby around in a wheelchair. I don't suppose it did him much good but they both enjoyed themselves and looked better for the change.

In the September Muriel and I went up North, Muriel to Halifax and Tony and me to Manchester for a week, then I went to Bruce and Ellie. The last Saturday we all went to Halifax to see the local operatic society's production of Gilbert and Sullivan's 'Patience'. We all enjoyed it very much. I certainly did, especially when I won first prize in the raffle. I have an idea Bruce won the second one. Tony and Barbara played a large part in the society's activities.

13

1997-2000

1997 started off very well. On the 19th of January I became a great-grandmother. Ruth and Euan had a lovely baby girl Jemma Louise.

In the beginning of March Muriel went into the Plymouth Eye Infirmary for a cataract operation. All went well and she came to me afterwards for a few days.

June was an exciting time. Bruce took Muriel and I back to our old school for a reunion. This was the first time we had been back for some years. I mentioned earlier that our orphanage was now Snaresbrook Crown Court. I was quite disappointed because I wanted to show Bruce our classrooms and dormitories but they weren't there any more. The whole of the inside had been gutted to make way for the different courts and offices. The chapel was the only remaining feature from the school. They had not been allowed to change that. We had a very nice service in the chapel. Bruce had never been to the school before. He was impressed with the building and grounds. He booked us into a small hotel in Woodford but we had our evening meal at the Eagle Hotel right opposite the school. This had, of course, been out of bounds for us as girls! On the Sunday Bruce took us to all our old haunts: the lovely house in Highams Park, but most surprising of all to the house where Grandma and Grandpa used to live, the house we went to after Dada died.

We thought we would never see that again. Talk about a nostalgic journey, that really was one. Muriel and I were thrilled to bits, especially when we told Bill about it.

At the end of the month Muriel had a second cataract operation. She did not have to wait long for that one. All went well and again she came to me after leaving hospital.

At the end of June Bill and Ruby went to Peterborough to spend a week or so with Derek and his family. Bill's granddaughter from Canada had come over with her family for a visit. Bill said it was grand meeting all his grandchildren and great-grandchildren again. He was not too well while he was away though. Soon after he came back it was obvious that something was wrong. He did not feel like doing their shopping or very much at all, so I did a lot for them. Ruby had not been shopping for some time. In the September Bill was admitted to our local hospital. He became very ill indeed and he passed away on the 22nd September. He had been suffering from prostate cancer but had not told anyone. What a dreadful loss that was to Muriel and I and a great sadness for Ruby and Derek. Bill was a father, brother and friend to us all. Everybody loved him, even some of the shopkeepers in Kingsbridge shed a tear when he died. Derek and Joan came down and they took Ruby back with them until Bill's funeral, which was two weeks later.

I was feeling really worn out by now so the family advised Muriel and I to have a break so we went

North to our families. Ruby said she would be quite alright on her own. Her friend in the house opposite said she would keep an eye on her. The day I came home I rang Ruby about seven in the evening and asked her if she was O.K. She said she was fine and just going to get her tea. I told her that Tony and Muriel would be round early in the morning. Muriel and Tony arrived just before me and when I got to the house I saw an ambulance outside the door. It appears when Muriel and Tony arrived the blinds and curtains were still drawn and when they got in they found Ruby lying on the floor. The sitting room looked as though a bomb had hit it. What happened we will never know. Anyway Ruby was alright and she flatly refused to go to hospital for a check up. She told us all to go away and leave her alone. I was loath to do this but she was so insistent I thought it best to do as she wanted. I rang two or three times that day to see if she was O.K. I arranged to meet her doctor the next morning at Ruby's house. When I got there she was on the floor again. I rang for the ambulance and this time they took her to hospital. She never came home again. A week later she was moved to a local nursing home. Muriel and I visited her regularly. The staff were very kind to her but she was so very unhappy. She missed her Bill dreadfully, all she wanted was to be with him.

That Christmas Muriel and I went to our families. I spent Christmas with Bruce, Ellie and Hazel and the New Year with Beryl and her family. Muriel went to Tony and Barbara.

In January 1998 Pam was diagnosed with breast cancer, she had a total mastectomy and made a complete recovery, but only after some scares over secondary infection, with serious anxiety about MRSA. In March Ruby passed away. It was a happy release for her, I think she just pined for her Bill. I know Muriel and I miss him dreadfully. It was very strange because the day Ruby died she told two of the residents she was going to die that day. It was almost as though she had made up her mind to do so.

In September Muriel and I went up to the Lake District with our families for the wedding of Neil and Jane. In the morning there was thunder and lightning but, in the afternoon, in time for the ceremony, the sun shone. The bride looked gorgeous, her two bridesmaids were her sisters. Neil's two brothers Euan and David and Jane's brother were ushers. The reception was held in a beautiful old hotel, where a number of us guests stayed the night and I enjoyed dancing in the disco until after midnight!

1999 was a proud year for me as Bruce was given a professorship. How proud I am of him. In fact I am proud of all my children and grandchildren. Also this year I got to know Hazel's boyfriend Guy, how happy I was for her.

At the end of this year I was told that Thora, my oesophageal tumour, was no longer responding to the alcohol treatment. So, in December, I spent two weeks at Derriford hospital for intensive radiotherapy. I still have the tattooed target on my throat! In January I was told by the oncologist that the tumour had disappeared. It has not returned and, as this was one of the most dangerous forms of cancer, I feel that I am one of the lucky ones!

14

2000-2006

After the anxiety then the relief of my cancer treatment, even though I have to go into hospital every three months to have my throat stretched, the early part of the year was uneventful. Muriel and I had more poems published and I wrote my first novel *The Wilders*, and a murder mystery *A most undignified death*, neither have been published but I just write for my own amusement and to keep my brain active.

Ruth and Euan gave me another great granddaughter, Beverley Jane, born on June 20th, a sister for Jemma.

On November 24th Muriel and I reached our 90th birthday, and of course we had to have a party! This took place in the Loddiswell village hall and over seventy guests came. The local hotel did the catering, there was a live band and we all danced. On our actual birthday we both had an appointment at the hair salon. When our coiffures were ready four gentlemen walked into the salon together with the town crier. Soon after a reporter from the *Kingsbridge Gazette* arrived. "Right," said Beverley, the hairdresser, "let the party begin." The town crier read a speech then the four men - the local barbershop quartet – sang to us. We all then enjoyed a glass of sherry and some cake. The reporter took photographs and interviewed us about our lives. It was exciting to be famous for a day and it all appeared in the next edition of the paper. Muriel and I will never forget what Beverley arranged to make our birthday so memorable. I felt so delighted when the surgeon who had been looking after me at Derriford accepted our invitation to the party. I was only sorry that my own GP, who had looked after me so well for so long, was out of the country. I owe so much to the medical profession!

During the year I had written about our life in the orphanage (the first chapters of this book.) One day Muriel rang to say that a film company in Bristol was asking people of our generation to let them known how our childhood was spent. I rang them and explained about my writing and they asked me to send them a copy. A few days later I had a phone call from the studio saying they really had to put some of the story on television as they had found it very moving. Eventually Muriel and I found ourselves in Bristol for the interviews and filming. It was quite an experience and everyone was very kind. In July 2001 we were on BBC2 as part of *A pocketful of posies* which was well received.

Just before Christmas 2001 something happened which changed my life. I woke one night with terrible pains in my legs. I jumped out of bed quickly, thinking it was cramp, but then my hand began to feel strange. After walking about for about for a while and stamping my feet the pain did not go away so I went back to bed. In the morning I rang my doctor. When he came he said that it could be muscular trouble. I told him I was going to Beryl the following week and then on to Bruce for the New Year. He said he would arrange a blood test when I came back. Two days later when I was shopping with Muriel I could hardly walk and my breathing was getting difficult. On reaching home I rang the doctor again. I could not see my own doctor but one of his colleagues again said that it was probably muscular.

When Beryl came to collect me she could see that something was wrong but we left for Manchester as planned. Little did I know that it would be the last time I would see my home. In Manchester things got worse. I was having great difficulty using the stairs so Beryl made me up a bed downstairs and borrowed a wheel-chair. Although I was feeling pretty poorly I tried not to let it spoil Christmas. After Boxing Day Beryl rang her own doctor who sent me to Manchester Royal Infirmary as an emergency case. The casualty doctor sent me to the Physiotherapy Department to acquire a Zimmer frame. The physiotherapist was unwilling to give me one without a proper diagnosis, so I was sent home. Two days later things had become so bad that Beryl rang her doctor again and at eleven o'clock that night I was off to the MRI once more. Eventually, at three in the morning, I saw a doctor who took blood tests and gave me an ECG test. I went home none the wiser and feeling even worse.

The next morning Beryl rang Bruce and the family had a council of war. It was becoming obvious to everyone that I needed to be looked after and they knew that they could not cope. I could hardly dress myself and needed help with everything, and I mean *everything!*

It was decided that the best place for me, where I could be properly looked after 24 hours a day, was a residential home. I know that this was as terrible a decision for them to take as it was for me to accept, but at the time I was feeling too ill to worry about it. Bruce was lucky enough to find, in just one day, a nice home in Hawarden. I was transferred to Bruce's doctor's list and he arranged for an x-ray at Mold hospital. All this showed was that I had some arthritis in my neck – it did not explain my inability to use my legs or hands. The doctor arranged for me to see a neurologist but there was a six-week wait on the NHS. We saw the same specialist privately in a few days. By now I had a gleam of an idea as to what my condition was but I said nothing.

I was becoming adjusted to life in Sycamore Lodge. I have a lovely big room with my own toilet and the staff are very kind and caring. At this stage I could do nothing for myself but I soon got over the embarrassment and saw the funny side of things. Bruce, Beryl and Gareth took me to the Nuffield Hospital in Chester to see the specialist who was kind and very understanding. After he had examined me I asked him if he thought I might have Guillain-Barré Syndrome. He looked at me in astonishment and asked why I thought that, as it is a very rare complaint. I then told him about my brother Frank and that I seemed to have the same symptoms. He arranged for me to be admitted to the new Walton Neurological Hospital in Liverpool for tests and Bruce took me there a few days later. Again the staff were wonderful, although some of the tests were very painful, but they confirmed my diagnosis! I was only in the hospital for four days but when I left I was able to walk a few steps again.

I was able to go for physio- and occupational therapy at the local community hospital and I was take every week by ambulance until I got some use back in my hands. I was still not able to walk much. I remember one night two carers helped me off the stair life and into my bedroom, but then my legs gave way and, amid a great deal of laughter, they dragged me across the room to my bed and hauled me up onto it. They started to undress me with the light full on and the curtains open. I asked them if they would kindly pull the curtains across before they had quite stripped me. "Oh no," they replied, "a bus will be along in a moment and we have paid the driver to stop so his passengers can be entertained." This helped to cheer me up. By now I was beginning to miss Muriel terribly and I know she was missing me.

While I was recovering Bruce put my house in Devon on the market, using the same agents from whom we had bought it over thirty years before. The same morning that the advert appeared in the local paper we were able to agree a sale. We all knew that I would never be going back because, apart from the Guillain-Barré, my eyesight was failing and I was already registered as being partially sighted. Bruce and Ellie cleared my house and Beryl's youngest son, David, was a great help to his Uncle Bruce.

After nearly four months in the wheelchair I decided that it was time I helped myself a bit more. I was doing well with the physiotherapy and occupational therapy at the clinic but I wanted to do more for myself. One morning when the carer brought me down on the stair-lift I told her to have the wheelchair ready as I was going to try to walk up four stairs. "Oh, Phyllis," she replied, "are you sure?" "No," I answered, "but I intend to try!" Very slowly I went up four stairs. I admit I was petrified, but I walked down again and got into the wheelchair. The look on the carer's face was worth all the effort. The following day I walked up eight stairs and soon after I dispensed with the wheelchair. When I saw the specialist next he looked up in astonishment to see me walking into his consulting room. He thought I would still be in the wheelchair. Soon afterwards I was discharged from the physiotherapy clinic.

One day during tea it suddenly struck me that I was never going to sleep in my own house again. I felt the tears coming and beckoned to Lisa, one of the carers. She could see how distressed I was and took me upstairs, then rang Bruce. Bless his heart, he was with me in twenty minutes. He told me that the family had been expecting this and that it was a natural reaction to the turmoil and anxiety of the last few months as well as the real sense of loss of my home. I soon cheered up and have not been upset since. Of course I now have the benefit of seeing my family frequently and they take me out and I can spend time with them in their homes. When I lived in Kingsbridge I saw them once or twice a year, now its twice a week or more.

In August Muriel moved to Bradford in Yorkshire to be near to near her son Tony and his ex-wife, Barbara. I suppose things worked out for the best although both Muriel and I were loath to say farewell to Devon and all the friends we had made in the more than thirty years we had lived there. In September Tony re-married, to Joan, and it was a very nice wedding and a wonderful chance to see all the members of the family again.

In October Gareth married Suzanne at Sychtyn Hall, near Mold, a lovely old house. About a hundred guests enjoyed a grand occasion and several of us stayed the night. The following first of March, St. David's Day, Hazel and Guy were married at Peckforton Castle in Cheshire. This is a mock castle but very well modernised as a comfortable hotel. Again it was a great opportunity for all the family to get together. I felt so proud to see Hazel looking so lovely as she came in on Bruce's arm. I admit I did shed a tear. Ralph would have been so proud to have seen his only grand-daughter looking so radiant.

On December 6th Hazel had a baby daughter, Lara Isabel Eva. Bruce and Ellie were delighted because, although Hazel and Guy had been living together for some time they did not want children until they were married. I admired them for this. To add to everyone's happiness Suzanne, who was spending New Year with Ellie and Bruce, gave birth to a son on January first. He should have been born in February and was born in the same hospital as his father, Gareth, and his cousin Lara. Benjamin Alexander Lewis-Ing was not only a surprise but a welcome addition to the clan. As Bruce said, they had waited years for grandchildren then two came along at once!

Hazel and Guy live a few minutes away in the same road as Sycamore Lodge so Hazel brings Lara to see me from time to time. She has become a great favourite with the staff and the other residents.

I am now the oldest inhabitant of the home, and hopefully not the village idiot, and I try to be as helpful as I can to staff and residents alike. When I go away to stay with Beryl or Muriel the staff say that it is too quiet without me. I wonder what they could mean! I must admit that I never thought that I would ever settle in a home after being brought up in an orphanage. However, I had not realised until I had been here for a while how lonely I was in Devon and how down I was, especially on Sundays.

Bruce and Tony took Muriel and me back to the Cottage Hotel at Hope Cove for two lovely holidays so that we could say our goodbyes to all our friends and see our favourite places again. Muriel is not a good traveller so we probably will not go again.

Since I have been at Sycamore Lodge Bruce has bought me an electric typewriter and a proper desk and chair so that I can continue with my writing. I have published a small book of poems about life in the home and some of the antics of my fellow residents. I visit Muriel quite often and really enjoy the route across the Pennines. Muriel has a weak heart and lungs but she is living by herself in a nice bungalow with good neighbours. She does her own cooking and washing still, but has help with cleaning and the garden.

In late 2004 it was discovered that I had cardiac arrhythmia and I would need a pacemaker. This has been fitted and is working well, so now I am a bionic woman! I still have to have my throat stretched from time to time – the treatment which destroyed the cancer damaged the lining of my oesophagus - and the pacemaker means that I can face the anaesthetic without risk.

Bruce and Ellie are planning to move to Scotland in late 2007. They have a beautiful house by the sea just outside Ullapool, in the far north-west. In May 2005 they took me for a holiday in the Highlands and on the way, we visited some of the places that Bruce had taken me and Ralph to in 1968. I really enjoyed sitting in the sunshine looking at the mountains, sea and islands from their garden. I know they will be happy there and I am glad for them.

We have now reached 2006 and two more happy events have occurred. Gareth and Suzanne had a daughter, Poppy Alice, in March, and Hazel and Guy had a son, James Cameron, in June. So now

I have six great-grandchildren. It seems odd that my own children are now grandparents, but they seem to be thriving on it.

I am very proud of all my grandchildren. Hazel is a professional oboist. She studied at Birmingham Conservatoire and then at the Conservatoire at Berne, in Switzerland. She has not been able to secure a permanent orchestral post but she taught the oboe at a variety of schools and had private pupils. She also plays in local orchestras and for theatre shows. She now teaches with Ellie at the local Further Education College. Her husband Guy is an architect with a firm in Wrexham.

Gareth had a chequered career as a salesman and decided to change direction. He took a home computer course and quickly found a progression of increasingly better jobs. He is now working for an international computer company and is living in a lovely village in Oxfordshire, on the edge of the Cotswolds. Suzanne, whom he met at Leicester University where she was a student, used to work for the Open University, until the children came along.

Euan studied Animal Biology at Nottingham University but then struggled to get a permanent job, so he trained as a teacher and is now happily teaching Science at a Manchester School and is also involved in school Drama productions. This is not too surprising as Beryl, after years as a Social Worker, also trained as a teacher and is soon to retire from a school in Stalybridge, where she teaches Science and helps with the Drama! Euan's wife Ruth was a dental technician but, with two lively girls, Jemma and Beverley, is not otherwise working at present. They also live in Manchester.

Neil studied Chemistry and Biochemistry at Salford University and has a very good job with Glaxo. He met his wife, Jane, who is a forensic chemist, while on work experience in Germany, in the Black Forest. They have recently moved to their own house near Glasgow.

David, my youngest grandchild, is still living at home with Beryl and Malcolm. He worked for many years for British Aerospace as an engineer and also spent much of his spare time organising fundraising for several childrens' charities. He went on walks with such personalities as Ian Botham. He has taken advantage of not being married by travelling round the world several times. At the time of writing (July 2006) he does not know where he will be working next. How different is the experience of the young today compared to my own youth!

This story has been about my family, our trials and tribulations, our tears and laughter. We are a resilient family and do not like to give in to difficulties. I have had a long and not always happy life but I am confident that the families that have grown from my children will live long and prosper. What more could I ask? Muriel and I are the only members of our generation left but we are looking forward to our centenary surrounded by our loved ones. No doubt there will be a few more tears ahead but I'm sure that when the time finally comes Muriel and I will greet St. Peter at the Pearly Gates, hand in hand, and still laughing!